SVANEMØLLEN

Yderhavnen

HOLMENS
KIRKEGÅRD

Kastellet

Lille Havfrue
(Little Mermaid)

Hirschsprungske
Samling

Statens
Museum
for Kunst

6

Geologisk
Museet

Rosenborg
Slot

KONGENS
HAVE

5

Davids
Samling

Amalienborg
Plads

Operaen

4

Post & Tele
Museum

Kongens
Nytorv

3

Vor Frue
Kirke

CHRISTIANS
HAVN

Holmens
Kirke

10

Christiansborg
Slot

Børsen

11

National-
museet
(National Museum)

Den Sorte
Diamant

Christians
Kirke

Vor Frelsers
Kirke

9

Carlsberg
Glyptoteket

KLØVERMARKEN

BRO

AMAGERBRO

SUNDBY
VESTER

CONTENTS

ABOUT THIS BOOK

Above: some of the attractions of Copenhagen.

This *Step by Step Guide* has been produced by the editors of Insight Guides, whose books have set the standard for visual travel guides since 1970. With top-quality photography and authoritative recommendations, this guidebook brings you the very best of Copenhagen in a series of 14 tailor-made tours.

WALKS AND TOURS

The tours provide something for all budgets, tastes and time spans. As well as covering Copenhagen's classic attractions – of which there are many – the routes track lesser-known sights, and there are also day excursions for those with both the time and inclination to explore slightly further afield.

The tours embrace a range of interests, so whether you are an art enthusiast, an architecture buff, a gourmet, a lover of flora and fauna, a historian or royalist, or have children to entertain, you will find an option to suit. For our pick of the walks by theme, consult Recommended Tours For… *(see pp.6–7).*

We strongly recommend that you read a tour before setting out. This should help you to familiarise yourself with the route and enable you to plan where to stop for food – options are shown in the 'Food and Drink' boxes, which are recognisable by the knife and fork sign, on most pages.

ORIENTATION

The tours are set in context by this introductory section, giving an overview of the city, plus information on food and drink, shopping and entertainment. A short history timeline in this chapter highlights the key events that have shaped Copenhagen over the centuries.

DIRECTORY

Supporting the tours is a Directory chapter, comprising a user-friendly, clearly organised A–Z of practical information, our pick of where to stay and select restaurant listings. The entries grouped under 'Restaurants' complement the more low-key cafés and eateries that feature within the tours, and are intended to offer a wider choice for evening dining.

The Author

Antonia Cunningham was educated at Cambridge University, where she studied Languages and Art History. Following a short stint as an A-level tutor, she turned her hand to publishing, where she found her way into travel editing and writing. She has written several books, including non-fiction for children, two books on world art and the Impressionists, and five on Copenhagen and Denmark, including Insight's *Smart Guide Copenhagen*. Every time she visits this friendly, walkable city she finds something new and is always charmed by it. She lives in London with her partner Nick and son Benjamin, to both of whom she dedicates this book.

Margin Tips
Shopping tips, handy hints, information on activities, key historical facts and interesting snippets help visitors make the most of their time in Copenhagen.

Feature Boxes
Notable topics are highlighted in these special boxes.

Key Facts Box
This box gives details of the distance covered on the tour, plus an estimate of how long it should take. It also states where the tour starts and finishes, and gives key travel information such as which days are best to do it or handy transport tips.

Route Map
Detailed cartography shows the tour clearly plotted with numbered dots. For more detailed mapping, see the pull-out map slotted inside the back cover.

Footers
Those on the left-hand page give the tour name, plus, where relevant, a map reference; those on the right-hand page usually show the main attraction on the double page.

Food and Drink
Recommendations of where to stop for refreshment are given in these boxes. The numbers prior to each restaurant/café name link to references in the main text. On city maps, restaurants are plotted.

The € signs at the end of each entry reflect the approximate cost of a three-course meal for one, without wine. These should be seen as a guide only. Price ranges, also quoted on the inside back flap for easy reference, are as follows:

€€€€   over 550dkk
€€€   400–550dkk
€€   250–400dkk
€   under 250dkk

SHOPPERS

Resist temptation in the department stores on Strøget (walk 2) and Kongens Nytorv (walk 3), the boutiques off Strøget, in Nørrebro (walk 7) and the independent artists and designer shops in Vesterbro (walk 1).

RECOMMENDED TOURS FOR...

DESIGN COPENHAGEN

Lap up serious modern design at Illums Bolighus on Strøget (walk 2). The SAS Royal Radisson is a design icon (walk 1) and the Design Museum has wonderful displays (walk 4).

FOOD AND WINE

Copenhagen has 10 Michelin-starred restaurants. Værnedamesvej (walk 7) is Copenhagen's gourmet food street, while Magasin du Nord (walk 3) offers an excellent food hall.

CHILDREN

Treat the kids to a trip to Tivoli (walk 9), day or night, and fascinate them at the zoo (walk 1), Experimentarium or the Akvarium (tour 13). Dazzle them at the Rosenborg and visit the crown jewels (walk 5).

PARKS AND GARDENS

You can't come to Copenhagen, especially the first time, without experiencing the gardens of Tivoli (walk 9). On a sunny day, take a break in Kongens Nytorv (walk 5), the Assistens cemetery or along the reservoirs (walk 7).

HANS CHRISTIAN ANDERSEN

Wander through his stamping ground around Kongens Nytorv and Nyhavn (walk 3), and visit the Bakkehuset (walk 8). See *The Little Mermaid* (walk 7) and visit the cathedral where his funeral was held (walk 2) and his grave (walk 7).

ART ENTHUSIASTS

You are spoilt for choice with the Statens Museum for Kunst (walk 6), the Ny Carlsberg Glyptotek and the National Museum (walk 9), the Thorvaldsens Museum (walk 10) and the Rosenborg (walk 5). Outside the city are world-class galleries Arken, Ordrupgaard and Louisiana (tour 13).

CHRISTIAN IV AND THE RENAISSANCE

Visit Rosenborg Castle (walk 5), the Round Tower, Trinity Church and Caritas Fountain (walk 2), Børsen (walk 10), Kastellet and Nyboder (walk 4), Christianshavn (walk 11) and Frederiksborg Castle (walk 5).

ROMANTIC COPENHAGEN

Take a stroll along the reservoirs (walk 7), wander through Christianshavn (walk 11) or head along the banks of the Sound (walk 4).

ROYALISTS

Follow in the steps of kings at Slotsholmen (walk 10), Rosenborg (walk 5), St Mary's Cathedral (walk 2), the Amalienborg (walk 4) and Roskilde (walk 12). For a little Royal shopping, visit Royal Copenhagen on Strøget (walk 2).

Krokodillegade

ORIENTATION

An overview of geography, customs and culture, plus illuminating background information on food and drink, shopping, entertainment and history.

OVERVIEW

Copenhagen is a pretty seaside city with a thriving nightlife, the sophisticated gastronomic and cultural offerings of a far larger city and a visible history going back 900 years. It supports plenty of big business and is the world's ninth richest city in terms of gross pay per capita.

Population Density
Denmark is the smallest yet most densely populated nation in northern Europe with a land area of just 43,000 sq km (16,630 sq miles). In Denmark there are over six times as many people per sq km as in neighbouring Sweden.

Copenhagen (København), the capital of Denmark, is located on the eastern side of Sjælland (Zealand), the largest of Denmark's 406 islands, with only the Øresund (Sound) separating it from Sweden. It was founded by Bishop Absalon in 1167, and these days, including its greater metropolitan area, is home to about 1.5 million of the country's estimated 5.45 million people. The smaller municipality of Copenhagen – made up of 15 districts that extend beyond the geographical scope of this book – accounts for approximately 510,000 inhabitants.

STRATEGIC LINK TO EUROPE

Connected by the south of Jutland to Germany, Denmark is the only Scandinavian country physically joined to the European mainland and, as such, is the bridge between Scandinavia and the rest of the continent. It is also literally the bridge to Sweden with the Øresund road and rail bridge linking it with the city of Malmö.

Consequently, Denmark shares many of the characteristics of its Nordic neighbours: liberal welfare benefits coupled with a high standard of living, and a style of government that aims at consensus and the avoidance of petty bureaucracy. Yet Denmark is also more 'European' and accessible than the rest of Scandinavia, and its appeal is universal.

THE CITY

With its strategic location at the mouth of the Baltic Sea, Copenhagen has always been an important hub and, as such, a tempting prize for pirates and traders. As a small fishing village in the 12th century, it attracted the protection of Bishop Absalon and the dastardly attentions of Wendish pirates. One century later, German traders of the Hanseatic League were pounding on its doors. By the 15th century, the Sound was even more of a cash cow with its herring salted and exported all over Europe and the king charging a toll on every ship that passed on its way to the Baltic.

Over the centuries, Copenhagen grew but always, even today, remained reasonably compact, its residents moving out gradually from the central conurbation. In the 12th century, Slotsholmen was the centre; by the Middle Ages, the town had expanded across the water to the banks of what is now the Old Town.

The medieval citizens put up walls surrounded by a moat, which enclosed the city to the north, east and west. With the exception of Østerport (East Gate), which stood on Gothersgade until the 17th century, near to what is now Kongens Nytorv, the gates in the walls were on or near the sites still called Nørreport (North Gate) and Vesterport (West Gate). The fortress of Slotsholmen and the watery boundary of the Sound stood to the south. The five reservoirs to the north are all that remain of the medieval moat.

In the 16th century, under the aegis of Christian IV, the city's fortifications were extended east. The fortress Kastellet *(see p.52)* was built, and the East Gate and rampart moved up near it, thus bringing Rosenborg (1606–34) within the walls and practically doubling the amount of space inside the city walls in what was known as 'New Copenhagen'. To the south, Christianshavn *(see p.82)* was built up and a series of new islands created with naval yards and protective bastions. Nyboder, near Østerport, was built to house the naval workers. At the same time, Christian IV created some of the most lasting buildings of the entire city; boasting an elegant Renaissance style, they are still standing today.

One century later, the city expanded again, as Frederiksstad *(see p.47)* was built in 'New Copenhagen' on the land acquired by Christian IV. It was (and is) the most aristocratic area in town, and was constructed on the site of a former royal country palace that had burnt down. On the banks of the Sound, Kongens Nytorv was developed and Nyhavn was excavated and the merchants built their houses along its wharfs, to be close to the precious goods in their warehouses.

Fire was always a threat in a town made of wood, and the 18th century saw two shocking blazes that destroyed almost the whole of the medieval centre. With the odd exception (including, fortunately, most of Christian IV's marvellous buildings), what the visitor sees today is 18th-century neoclassical architecture.

By the 19th century, Copenhagen was too compact: it was packed with people and had no sanitation to speak of; certainly not enough to deal with the effluence that the heaving city spat out daily. In 1853, cholera broke out, killing several thousand people, including the well-known Golden-Age artist, Christoper Eckersberg.

In 1856, the old ramparts were pulled down to improve conditions and the populace spread into the countryside, which soon became the

Above from far left: Søndre Frihavn, north of the city; royals from all over Europe turned up for the wedding of Crown Prince Frederik with Mary Donaldson in May 2004.

Café Culture
Sitting out in a café is an indisputable part of the modern Copenhagen experience, but Copenhagen's first continental-style café, Café Sommersko, did not open until 1976.

Below: buzzing cafés in front of the multicoloured houses in Nyhavn.

Above from left: the unmistakable façade of the Palads Theatre, in Axeltorv; Danes are keen cyclists; the city is dotted with beautiful, peaceful gardens.

districts of Nørrebro, Vesterbro, Østerbro and Frederiksberg (although this is still technically a separate municipality from Copenhagen).

Thanks to the architect and town planner Ferdinand Meldahl (1827–1908), these districts were conserved as the parks that ring the inner city today, stretching from Kastellet, via Østre Anlaeg behind the National Museum of Art, the Botanical Gardens and Ørsteds Parken. Tivoli, also once part of the ramparts, was the work of entrepreneur George Carsten in 1843 *(see p.75)*.

COPENHAGEN TODAY

The 21st century has seen further changes to the city, particularly the pedestrianisation of the old quarter. The docks are being rejuvenated and the authorities have taken a particular interest in updating the city's landscape with startling modern buildings such as the Black Diamond and the Opera House.

Below: sailing out of the harbour.

Copenhagen Districts

As in most large cities, different areas can be categorised by the sort of people (and incomes) that tend to populate them; these, of course, change over time as areas come and go in terms of popularity and economic upkeep.

Briefly, Indre By, the inner city covering an area of 4.65 sq km (1,150 acres), including the Old Town, is becoming less and less populated. Just 26,000 people live here, 6,800 of them in the Old Town, mostly near the cathedral and in Pisserenden (the unofficial name for the streets around Sankt Peders Stræde); fewer than 500 live in the financial district behind Kongens Nytorv and Holmens Kanal.

There are generally more visitors snoring away gently every night than there are locals. More than half the apartments in this area are lived in by affluent single people; few families stay, moving out to the suburbs where they can have a house and a garden for the kids. Many of the inhabitants are now in the 50-plus age bracket, newly moved in with the kids off their hands, wanting to be close to the cultural opportunities on offer. Typically, people live in flats on the top floor, above shops and businesses.

Students and young families tend to live in Nørrebro or Vesterbro, which are also Copenhagen's most multicultural areas. Nørrebro has a population of just over 31,000 and is the second most densely populated district after elegant Frederiksberg *(see p.67)*. In recent years, it has seen more social problems than other parts of the city;

nonetheless, it has the reputation for being a trendy and cool place to hang out. Vesterbro, once very seedy, is now respectably edgy and becoming more popular, especially with a young and creative crowd.

Christianshavn is Copenhagen's little Amsterdam, surrounded by water; according to one commentator, it was 'built for rich people, taken over by poor people and is now radical chic', although there are plenty of affluent newcomers, resented by the locals, who are attracted by its regeneration.

Østerbro and Frederiksberg are more upmarket; there are several embassies in Østerbro, including those of the US, Canada, Great Britain and Russia.

AN ECO-FRIENDLY CITY

These days, Copenhagen is still a compact city and, for the visitor, eminently walkable or bicycle-friendly. The Danes cycle in their thousands: men in suits, mums with babies in cart extensions, people cycling with pets, as well as the students and the younger generation. It makes for a city with clear air, few traffic jams, an impression of safety and a satisfying sense of doing something for the planet, which plays a large part in most Copenhageners' psyche.

Being eco-friendly is no idle desire; 35 per cent of the city's traffic is pedal-powered and there are 300km (186 miles) of bike paths with plans to create more. There are also special carriages for bikes on trains to enable cyclists to combine biking with travelling on public transport more easily.

The emphasis on being eco-friendly becomes clear fairly quickly, from the wind farms in the Sound (incidentally, awarded a Blue Flag and clean enough to swim in), visible as you fly in to the airport or look up the Sound from the Little Mermaid, to the bikes and organic revolution that is taking place in Copenhagen's restaurants. In the latter, the authorities are taking a strong part, ordaining that 90 per cent of all food served in the city's public institutions will be organic by 2015. Copenhagen also has a very ambitious programme of recycling, with plans to limit non-recyclable materials to two per cent of household waste.

Wind Farms
The wind farms on the Sound power 40,000 Copenhagen homes, and in Denmark overall, turbines supply 14 per cent of all electricity.

The Danes

Copenhagen's inhabitants are as appealing as their city; liberal, generally law-abiding, socially responsible (just look at their generous social security system, paid for with huge taxes that no-one seems to complain about), gregarious, and – at the same time – charming and sarcastic. They are skilled at enjoying life, especially when it comes to enjoying *hygge*, a word that loosely translates as a combination of warmth, well-being and intimacy, usually involving the combination of family, friends, food and copious amounts of alcohol. They are also informal in dealing with people and put a lot of focus on their personal freedom.

FOOD AND DRINK

Twenty years ago, a trip to Copenhagen may not have yielded significant gastronomic pleasure unless you were keen on herring. That has changed and Copenhagen boasts the most Michelin stars of any city in Scandinavia.

The Local Hooch
Aquavit *(akvavit),* the local spirit that is usually flavoured with caraway seed, is cheaper than imported spirits.

Traditional Danish food, as you would expect from a seafaring nation in a cold, murky climate, was based around sturdy, filling dishes of carbohydrates, meat and fish.

A generally agricultural and seafaring nation, people produced food from what they grew themselves or was available locally, using ingredients such as apples, beer, bread, cereals, carrots, dairy products, pork, onions, plums, potatoes and seafood. Dishes were seasonal in spring and summer but in the long, cold, dark winters, dishes depended on ingredients that had been preserved from the harvest seasons, using techniques such as pickling and salting. In the days of no refrigeration, it was these foods – ones that could be stored almost indefinitely – that came to dominate the fleeting pleasures of fresh fruit and vegetables, which barely feature in traditional dishes.

These days, Danish food, especially in restaurants, has lightened up a bit. With more contact with foreign cultures and food through holidays, immigration and greater food marketing and availability, the Danes, like the inhabitants of much of the rest of Europe, have become increasingly familiar with foreign dishes and ingredients. Leading the way is a generation of young chefs who are grasping the opportunity to combine Danish dishes and flavours with ingredients from abroad to create a new 'fusion' cuisine (especially French, Italian and Thai), so producing a new angle and perception of traditional food from different cultures. There is also an ever-increasing emphasis on seasonal, fresh and oft-times organic produce to create healthy, simple dishes.

DAILY MEALS

A traditional Danish breakfast, or *Morgenmad,* involves bread and butter, cheese, possibly cold meats and coffee. Porridge and beer-and-bread porridge *(Øllebrød)* are also very occasionally eaten. Of course, many people also eat cereal. Coffee is generally drunk rather than tea. In a hotel, the sheer scope of choice can be overwhelming, especially if faced with plates and plates of small Danish pastries *(wienerbrød).*

Lunch, or *Frokost,* can vary, but most people have an open sandwich or *smørrebrød.* This is traditionally a piece of dark rye bread with a topping. These can be quite complicated: *Dyrlægens natmad* ('Veterinarian's midnight snack'), for example, consists of liver paté *(leverpostej),* topped with corned beef *(salt kød)* and a slice of meat aspic *(sky),* plus raw onion rings and cress.

Other traditional sandwich toppings include smoked eel, scrambled egg and radishes; chopped liver paté with bacon and sauteed mushrooms; thin slices of roast pork *(ribbensteg)* with red sweet and sour cabbage; *gravadlax* (slices of smoked or cured salmon on white bread with shrimp, lemon and fresh dill); and, perhaps most complex of all, *Stjerneskud* ('Shooting Star'), which consists of two pieces of fish (one steamed, one fried and battered) on a piece of buttered white bread, piled high with shrimp, mayonnaise, red caviar and a slice of lemon.

A traditional alternative to *smørrebrød*, is to eat from a *Dansk Kold Bord*, or Danish Cold Table. Some restaurants offer these, though it is very typical at home on festive occasions. The cold table is like a buffet, with a cold first course, usually some sort of marinated herring *(marinerede sild)*, which might be pickled or served up in a red or white vinegar dressing. Sour cream sauces are also popular. On extra festive occasions, the herring might be prepared with other ingredients, such as potato, onions and capers topped with a dill sour cream/mayonnaise sauce. Herring is usually served with ice-cold *snaps*, which, according to the Danes, helps it to swim down to the stomach. The high level of alcohol also helps aid digestion.

The second course will be cold meats and salads, followed by a warm dish *(see box right)*, usually on a piece of rye bread, followed by cheese and biscuits.

Supper is called *Middag* because it used to be eaten in the middle of the day. It is eaten at home and most Danes make an effort to gather the family around a hot meal every evening. Meat is usually served, often with traditional gravy and potato dishes, although international foods, such as pasta, pizza and American-influenced foods are also popular.

Above from far left: chefs at work; Danes love their berries; a feast for the eyes and the tastebuds.

Traditional Dishes

Æbleflæsk	Pork slices with an apple, onion and bacon compote.
Æggekage	'Egg cake': a substantial omelette-like dish made with flour so it rises slightly.
Biksemad	Beef hash served with a fried egg and ketchup.
Blodpølse	Black pudding, made from pig's blood.
Brændende Kærlighed	Called 'Burning Love', this is mashed potato with fried onion and pieces of bacon *(pictured below)*.
Finker	Sweetmeat similar to haggis.
Flæskesteg	Roast pork with crackling *(svær)*.
Frikadeller	Meatballs, Denmark's 'national' dish.
Millionbøf	Tiny pieces of beef in gravy, poured over mashed potato. The name means 'million steak'.
Øllebrød	Porridge made of rye bread, sugar and beer.
Stegte sild i eddike	Fried herring in vinegar.

EATING AT HOME

Food plays an important part both in the Danish psyche, as it brings people together, and in the concept of 'hygge', a term hard to translate but meaning something along the lines of 'cosiness, warmth and comfort with good food, drink and company' although it can mean different things to different people. As such, eating together is an important social event, whether it is a daily family affair or a dinner with non-family guests.

As in most places, there are traditional times of year that the family comes together if it can. In Denmark, a Christmas lunch (*Julefrokost*) and an

Traditional Supper Until the mid-20th century, two courses were served: a first course, such as gruel, meat broth or sweet fruit soup, and a main course of meat or fish, always accompanied by potatoes and gravy.

Below: Danish-style food presentation.

Easter lunch *(Påskefrokost)* are traditional. The Christmas table or *Julebordet* is organized like a *Kold Bord*, and, in addition to everyday *smørrebrød* toppings, there will be special Christmas dishes such as *æbleflæsk* (pork slices served with an apple, onion and bacon compote), *flæskesteg* (roast pork with crackling) and *Jule sylte*, a pork paté served with pickled beetroot and mustard.

Other traditional foods include goose (though many people now prefer duck), eaten on 24 December with boiled potatoes, pickled red cabbage, tiny caramelised potatoes and gravy and, for pudding, *Ris à l'amande*, a rice pudding served with whipped cream, chopped almonds and cherry sauce. Traditionally, everyone eats until someone finds a whole almond. This dish was served first as, in the past, it was used to fill everyone up, so that a small amount of meat would go around (rather like English Yorkshire pudding, which is now served alongside the meat but used to be served first). The meal is usually washed down with beer or *snaps*.

EATING IN RESTAURANTS

Eating out is not a typically Danish occupation, although it is becoming increasingly popular, especially in cities and among the young and those with a disposable income.

In Copenhagen, there are over 2,000 restaurants and cafés, which will usually provide a good meal. There are also those that will provide something

extraordinary as indicated by the city's eight restaurants with nine Michelin stars awarded between them in 2007. **Noma**, the Scandinavian restaurant in Christianshavn is the proud possessor of a second star.

Copenhagen's cafés are usually open from the morning until late at night and most serve alcohol and will provide food throughout the day and into the evening. Some turn into clubs with music and dancing at night.

Restaurants are usually a bit more formal and the kitchen will close a couple of hours before the last people are expected to leave. If you want to eat late, always ring to find out when the kitchen closes. Restaurants that serve both lunch and supper will have a quiet period in the late afternoon when they will stop serving, so don't be surprised if lunch is not available after about 2pm. For smart restaurants, it is always advisable to book ahead.

WHERE TO BUY FOOD

If you want to buy food yourself, Copenhagen has some excellent food stores. Dubbed a 'gourmet street', Vesterbro's **Værnedamsvej** is a wonderful place to find high-quality butchers, greengrocers, wine, cheese and chocolate shops. If you don't get that far, all the department stores are generally worth a visit for their upmarket grocers.

For organic bread, patisserie, wine, chocolate and oil check out one of the **Emmerys** stores (Østergade 51; Vesterbrogade 34; Store Strandstraede

2; www.emerys.dk). There is also something of a new wave in organic delicatessens: **Meyers Deli** (Kongens Nytorv 13; Gammel Kongevej 107; www.meyersdeli.dk) and **Taste Please** (H.C. Andersens Boulevard 12; tel: 36 14 02 01; www.lantz.dk) are both central, new and offer all sorts of delicious goodies; Meyers also offers meals to eat in or take away. On the same street, you can also find Copenhagen's first organic supermarket, **Egefeld** (Gammel Kongevej 113; www.egefeld.dk), while near the Rosenborg, there is another attractive organic café, **Verde Food & Coffee** (Nørre Farimasgade 72), where you can eat and pick up your emails at the same time.

Eco-Labelling

The Danish mark of inspection for organic products is a red 'Ø' symbol. This indicates that the product has been inspected by the Danish authorities and must meet stringent quality and production regulations. A product can only be marketed as organic if 95 percent of its ingredients are certified by the 'Ø' symbol. The swan symbol is the Nordic Council of Ministers eco-mark, which is used in the Nordic countries while the flower is the EU's official eco-label used throughout Europe. When you buy a product labelled with either a swan or a flower, you know that the product has been manufactured with the least possible impact to the environment, that the quality and functionality is just as good as other products and that it does not contain any toxic ingredients.

Above from far left: Danish blue cheese; Danish pastries; cafés usually open from morning until late at night.

Organic Commitment
The Danes are committed to organic and eco-friendly goods. Currently, in the private sector in Copenhagen, 10–12 per cent of goods bought are organic, and in the public sector, a world-record of 45 per cent of all food eaten in the city's public institutions is organic. Copenhagen has set itself targets for organic food consumption to be up to 90 per cent by 2015 in all of the city's public institutions. The target for purchases and consumption in the private sector (covering both private business and the home) is expected to reach at least 20 per cent

SHOPPING

Copenhagen is an appealing, if not wildly cheap, place to shop, especially for Danish designer goods, particularly furniture, household items and clothing. Whether you buy or not, it's a great place for window-shopping.

Tax-Free Shopping
If you make large purchases in tax-free stores, you will be able to reclaim your tax – a welcome bonus in a city that isn't the cheapest, but where home quality is usually very good.

If you are planning to wander at will and buy on spec, there are several areas that you might like to visit.

THE SHOPPING MAP

In the centre of town, Strøget is generally good for mainstream goods of varying prices. The quality of goods improves as you head up the street from Rådhuspladsen, reaching a rather smart conclusion up by Kongens Nytorv, with designer boutiques and furriers such as Chanel, Gucci, Sand and Birger Christiansen.

Amagertorv is home to the designer department store Illums, its sister store, Illums Bolighus, which will fulfill all your designer desires for household gadgets and wonderful streamlined Danish furniture and lighting, Royal Copenhagen for its world-famous china (and the opportunity to paint your own, *see p.36*) and Georg Jensen, the father of simply designed silver jewellery (at a price). Magasin du Nord, another smart department store located on Kongens Nytorv should look after many of your sartorial needs.

Do not be afraid to wander off Strøget into the streets adjoining and parallel to it, as it is here that you will find lots of independently owned, quirky little shops.

Farvergade, which runs east of Strøget into Kompagnistræde and Laederstræde in one uninterrupted pedestrian street, is lined with shops dealing in oriental rugs, antique furniture, silverware, china and curios. The prices aren't exactly low, but on a good day it's possible to find a fair deal. These streets are more popular than Strøget among Copenhageners and the cafés are always full of people.

On Laederstræde, check out Grøn-lykke (No. 3) for funky and kitsch home furnishings; tiny Stilleben opposite at No. 14 for lovely, hand-made porcelain ceramics and, hidden away in a basement next door at No. 5, Wettergren and Wettergren, whose owners update vintage clothing and accessories.

The Latin Quarter, close to the university, is home to several book shops *(boghandel)* and second-hand clothing and record shops.

At Købmagergade 7, make sure to visit the heavenly Jane Burchard textile handbag shop, housed in an old glove shop still with its historical fittings; it sells handmade baroque creations that really ought to be teamed with a huge dress, décolleté and diamonds.

Delightful baby clothes and toys can be found at Crème de la Crème à la Edgar at Kompagnistræde 8.

There is also a market on Gammel Strand (Sat–Sun 8am–2pm) and flower stalls round the back of Magasin du Nord. For a very exotic floral experience (though, astonishingly they charge to let you in), have a look in the window of designer florist Tage Andersen at Ny Adelgade 12.

Away from the Centre

Elsewhere, there are plenty of other opportunities, again mainly of an independent variety. Out in Nørrebro, for example, around Sankt Hans Torv, you will find plenty of antique and bric-a-brac shops on Ravensborggade, vintage clothing on Blågardsgade and eclectic, young clothing shops in streets such as Elmegade, radiating out from Sankt Hans Torv.

Nansensgade near the reservoirs is an up-and-coming area, with a smattering of interesting shops and cafés. For some of the best-priced, individual leather handbags in town, make sure you visit Carioca, located at No. 86 (tel: 45 93 41 81).

Istedgade in Vesterbro is also home to several boutiques run by young artists and designers still experimenting with their styles. Montre at Halmtørvet 19 brings many of their workshops and showrooms together under one roof.

Also check out Gustus at Istedgade 67B, a wonderful shop full of beautiful glass objects at reasonable prices, hand-blown by its Polish owner.

If you are after authentic antiques, Bredgade near the Amalienborg is full of shops and auction houses.

DANISH HOUSEHOLD DESIGN

Danish furniture ranks among the world's best. Here you'll see items credited to the designer rather than to the factory. Furniture is a national pride and most good pieces will have a black circular 'Danish Furniture-Makers' sticker attached. Lamps are also lovingly designed, as are household textiles and hand-woven rugs. The best stores for interior furnishings are Illums Bolighus, Casa (Store Regnegade 2; www.casagroup.com) and, north of Osterbrø, the designer furniture store, Paustian (Kalkbrænderiløbskaj 2; www.paustian.dk).

Scandinavian knives and tableware are also of the highest standard, and Zwilling J.A. Henckels (Vimmelskaftet 47; www.zwilling.com) on Strøget has by far the widest and most interesting array of cookware and kitchen utensils.

ENTERTAINMENT

There is lots to do in the evenings in Copenhagen, above and beyond eating out. This list offers the main venues, including two ground-breaking clubs, but there are always new places popping up (especially on the clubbing scene), so chat to the locals if you want to find out what's new and hip.

Above: Rust has live acts and plenty to drink.

Royal Danish Playhouse
The Royal Danish Playhouse is the newest addition to the Copenhagen cultural and architectural scene. On the waterfront near Nyhavn, it provides a visual, modern balance to the opera house a little further up the Sound opposite the Amalienborg. Almost half the building is constructed in the water, partly on new fill and partly on detached piles.

TIVOLI

An evening visit to **Tivoli** *(see p.75)* is a must, even if it is just for a wander to take in the lights, fireworks and the atmosphere. If you wish to be a little more focussed, the open-air stage has free evening concerts on Fridays. There is also an impressive new concert hall *(see below)*.

CONCERT HALLS

The **Tivoli Concert Hall** (tel: 33 15 10 12) is one of the largest classical venues for ballet, opera and classical music in Copenhagen; it also puts on rock concerts and is a major venue during the jazz festival in July. You will need to book in advance.

Another concert hall, the **Concert House** (Koncerthuset; Emil Holms Kanal 20; tel: 35 20 30 32; www.dr.dk/koncerthuset) on Amager is under construction and due to open in 2009. The building, designed by Frenchman Jean Nouvel, promises to be striking.

THEATRE, OPERA AND DANCE

There are several places on offer – some more dependent on an under-standing of Danish than others. The **Opera House** (Operaen; Ekvipage-mestervej 10, Holmen; tel: 33 69 69 69; *see p.87*) is a wonderful evening out offering both traditional and modern opera and ballet in a startling building. The auditorium is very comfortable with excellent visibility and acoustics. Ticket prices vary but can start from as little as 27dkk for a concert and 75dkk for an opera. Top prices rarely rise beyond 690dkk.

Its sister venue, the **Royal Theatre** (Det Kongelige Teater; tel: 33 69 69 69; www.kglteater.dk) puts on classic and contemporary drama, opera and dance across three spaces, the **Old Stage** (Den Gamle Scene; Kongens Nytorv), the **New Stage** (Stærekassen; Tordenskjoldsgade 5) and finally the **Turbine Halls** (Turbine Hallerne; Adelgade 10).

In addition, the **Danish Royal Playhouse**, Det Kongelige Teater og Kapel, (Kvæsthusbroen; tel: 33 69 69 33; www.kgl-teater.dk) has recently opened on the waterfront near Nyhavn. It has two stages – a large one with 750 seats and a smaller one with 250 seats – together with a restaurant, café and a large public square in front of the building with a view of the rest of the harbour area. For some performances

the north wall can be opened up on to the quayside.

The **New Theatre** (Det Ny Teater; Gammel Kongevej 29; 33 25 50 75; www.detnyteater.dk) just off Vesterbrogade does a roaring trade in big musicals such as West Side Story, My Fair Lady, Phantom of the Opera, The Producers and Chicago.

JAZZ CLUBS AND DINNER-DANCES

The **Copenhagen Jazz House** (Niels Hemmingsens Gade 10; tel: 33 93 26 16; ww.jazzhouse.dk) is recommended for modern jazz and offers an eclectic programme. Artists range from international names to young Danish jazz musicians. It has a bar upstairs and a large dance floor downstairs. There are 3–5 performances per week.

Another exciting jazz venue is **Mojo's** (Løngangsstræde 21C; tel: 33 11 64 53; booking 23 44 97 77; www.mojo.dk), an intimate place, known for its laid-back blues and live jazz. Its cosy and intimate and you should book ahead.

If you fancy an all-in-one glamorous bit of entertainment, try out **Wallmans Saloner** (Cirkusbyningen, Jernebanegade 8; tel: 33 16 37 00; www.wallmans.dk; Wed–Sat (Tue–Sat, Nov–Dec), from 6pm; show 7pm–11.15pm; nightclub 11.15pm–3am; Mon–Fri from 575dkk, Sat–Sun 695dkk), where your evening takes in a four-course meal and entertainment on seven stages as you eat, followed by a night of dancing.

CLUBS AND DISCOS

Copenhagen has plenty of clubs and places to dance the night away, including many cafés and bars. But for the really cool stuff check out **Rust** (8 Guldbergsgade, Norrebrø; tel: 35 24 52 00; www.rust.dk; Wed–Sat 9pm–5am; 50dkk, free Thur, over-21 in the nightclub and live bands after 11pm; concerts: charge) and **VEGA** (Enghavevej 40, Vesterbro; tel: 33 25 70 11; Fri–Sat 11pm–5am; free before 1am; concerts: charge). Rust is in the forefront of the city's music and clubbing scene, showcasing upcoming live acts and top international DJs, and VEGA offers several venues, a great atmosphere and an impressive list of top international acts and DJs.

Masken Bar and Café (Studiestræde 33; tel: 33 91 09 37; www.maskenbar.dk; Sun–Thur 4pm–1am, Fri 4pm–5am, Sat 3pm–5am) is a relaxed and friendly gay and lesbian venue, where you'll have little problem chatting to the locals.

HISTORY: KEY DATES

An expanding and contracting economic and political power, Denmark has, in its time, ruled over much of Europe and Scandinavia. It is now an independent-minded member of the EU.

Above: Viking ship; Bishop Absalon.

VIKING PERIOD

*c.*AD**700–1000**	The Vikings colonize Britain, Normandy and much of southern Sweden, and also reach Greenland, Canada, North Africa, Russia and Constantinople.
986	Harald Bluetooth converts to Christianity.

MIDDLE AGES

1157	Valdemar I accedes to the throne and unifies Denmark after a century of unrest.
*c.***1160**	Bishop Absalon builds the first castle on Slotsholmen.
1254	Købmandshavn (Copenhagen) receives a charter. The German Hanseatic League recognises its important role in Baltic trade.
1282	The nobles force Erik V to sign the Great Charter at Nyborg, agreeing to share power.
1340	Accession of Valdemar Atterdag (1340–75) who reinforces royal power and expands its territories.
1397	Margrethe I (1375–1412) sets up the Kalmar Union, an alliance with Norway and Sweden, in which Denmark rules all three.
1417	Margrethe's grandnephew, Erik VII, builds Kronberg Castle at Helsingør, a fortress and 'toll booth' to collect money from ships passing through the Sound.
1425–79	Copenhagen flourishes and grows. In 1443, it becomes Denmark's capital and in 1479, Copenhagen University is founded.

Old Ruins
The foundations of Slotsholmen Castle are considered the most important ruins in the capital today. You can see them now beneath Christiansborg Palace in the centre of Copenhagen.

RENAISSANCE

1523–34	The Kalmar Union ends with Gustav Vasa's coronation as King of Sweden. Norway remains part of Denmark until 1814.
1536	The Reformation: Denmark becomes a Protestant country.
1588–1648	Copenhagen booms and the city expands in the reign of Christian IV but Denmark's entry (1525–29) into the 30 years war

(1618–48) against Sweden is a disaster and leads to the loss of much Danish land. Denmark's prosperity slumps.

1648–70 Denmark fights and loses another war with Sweden, ceding a third of its territories. The Sound becomes the country border.

1665 Frederik III establishes an hereditary absolute monarchy.

Above from far left: Copenhagen on the map; the Øresund bridge links Denmark to Sweden.

18TH AND 19TH CENTURIES

1711–12 Plague claims a third of Copenhagen's population.

1728 and 1795 Major fires gut much of the city leading to reconstruction.

1754–1800s The Danish Academy of Art is founded, inspiring a 'Golden Age' (1800–50) of the arts. Serfdom is abolished in 1788.

1801–14 Neutral Copenhagen is bombarded by the English Navy to prevent her from doing business with France. Britain attacks again in 1807. The Danes side with France and is bankrupt by 1813. Denmark loses Norway to Sweden in the Treaty of Kiel.

1848–9 Frederik VII abolishes absolute monarchy.

1864 After war with Prussia and Austria, Denmark cedes her territories of Schleswig and Holstein to Germany.

20TH AND 21ST CENTURIES

1914–18 Denmark remains neutral during the First World War.

1929–40 Welfare state is set up under a left-wing coalition dominated by the Social Democrats. Economic depression in the 1930s.

1940–45 Neutral Denmark is invaded by Germany in 1940. It joins the Allies in 1943 and the Resistance takes most of the Jewish population to safety in Sweden. Britain liberates Denmark in 1945.

1968–71 Christiania is founded after student unrest.

1972 Margrethe II becomes queen. Denmark joins the EEC (EU).

1989 Denmark is the first country to recognise same-sex marriages.

1998 Denmark signs the Amsterdam Treaty coming closer to integration with Europe.

2000 Denmark votes against the euro. The Øresund Bridge, a rail and road link with Sweden, opens.

2001 Right-wing coalition unexpectedly takes power.

2006 *Jyllands-Posten* causes offence to the Muslim world by publishing 12 cartoons depicting the Prophet Muhammed.

2007 Rioting in Copenhagen results from the destruction by the authorities of the 'Youth House', a culture centre for leftist youth. Weeks later, a survey finds Copenhagen the happiest place in the EU.

CoBrA
A group of artists set up the abstract movement CoBrA (Copenhagen-Brussels-Amsterdam), painting in a Baroque-like surreal style with emphasis on brushwork and colour. Its leading exponent was painter Asger Jorn (1914–73); others included Pierre Alechinsky and Karel Appel.

WALKS AND TOURS

1

VESTERBRO

This walk takes you from Central Station through Vesterbro, an area that was built up in the 19th century and soon became home to the red light district. It has been rejuvenated in part but still retains an edge and is unlike the clean-cut Copenhagen that you find elsewhere.

Vesterbro

Vesterbro literally means 'West Bridge'; the west bridge crossed the city moat (the remains of which are the reservoirs that run from Vesterbro up to Østerbro, 'East Bridge') to the West Door or 'Vesterport' into the city.

DISTANCE 5km (3 miles)
TIME A half/full day
START Høvedbanegården
END Bakkehuset
POINTS TO NOTE

This is quite a lengthy walk. If you want to speed things up and possibly combine with all or part of the Frederiksberg Walk *(see p.67)*, after Værnedamsvej, take a 6A bus down Vesterbro to Pile Allé (turn left for Carlsberg) or on to the zoo.

Until the mid-19th century, Vesterbro-gade, Vesterbro's main street, was the paved and busy road that led to Copenhagen's west gate, or 'Vester-port', through a country area mainly put to pasture with a few industrial buildings and timber yards. Until 1853, building outside the city walls was not allowed except with express permission. However, with the rise of industrialisation, dreadful sanitation, increased pressure on living space within the city walls and a cholera out-break in June 1853, which killed

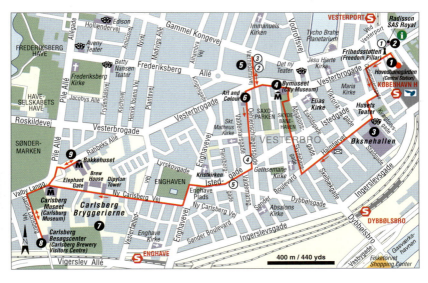

around 4,500 people, this prohibition was lifted. In 1856, the city ramparts and gates were pulled down, and there was no longer a barrier between the city and the land beyond. Building began in earnest in all the 'bro' ('bridge') districts beyond the city.

Vesterbro was never an expensive area and when the red-light district in Pisserenden was cleared out in the early 1900s, many of its 'workers' came to Vesterbro. There is still a red-light district here, but it is contained in a few streets, and the area is better represented by the resident immigrant population and the young artists and designers who also favour the area.

In the past, living conditions here have been poor; there are still some problems but gentrification has begun to set in and restoration and improvements have been made. Nonetheless, if you are wondering where the grittier side of life is to be found in Copenhagen, you will find some of it here.

OUTSIDE THE STATION

Start outside **Høvedbanegården ❶**, built in 1847–8 to serve Denmark's first railway line, which ran between Copenhagen and Roskilde *(see p.88)*. Look left, and in the middle of the road you will see an obelisk, the **Freedom Pillar** (Frihedstøtten).

The Freedom Pillar
Unveiled in 1797, when it stood outside the city walls, the Freedom Pillar commemorates the end of adscription in 1788, which meant that peasants

could leave the estate where they were born and choose to live and work elsewhere. Before this, they were legally tied to their feudal lord and could be hunted down, brought back and punished severely if they tried to leave. The four figures represent Loyalty, Civic Virtue, Cultivating the Soil and Valour.

Radisson SAS Royal Hotel
The tower block on the corner of Vesterbrogade and Hammerichsgade is the **Radisson SAS Royal Hotel ❷**, an icon in the history of architecture erected in 1960 by Arne Jacobsen (1902–71), the architect/designer credited with almost single-handedly creating the world's concept of practical but stylish and elegant Danish design. **Room 606** is the only one that retains Jacobsen's original design; if it's not booked and you ask nicely at reception, you might be able to see it. If you are hungry or would just like a marvellous view of the city, head up to the **Alberto K**, see ⓧ①, on the 20th floor for breakfast.

Above from far left: the sweeping view from the Alberto K restaurant; trendy Vesterbro bar; outside Hotel Axel on Helgolandsgade.

Swans and Eggs
Arne Jacobsen was involved in every aspect of the Radisson SAS Royal Hotel's design, even down to the door handles and cutlery. In the lobby you will see the famous 'Egg' and 'Swan' chairs, designed especially for this hotel more than 45 years ago.

Independent Shops and Cafés

Vesterbro is popular with young designers and you will come across some quirky, unusual shopping as you do this walk; the second-hand stores are also good and Café Vinyl, on Skydebanegade, a tiny coffeehouse with hardly any seating and lots of vinyl records, is a good example of the way some places in Copenhagen fuse their owner's personal enthusiams with a retail enterprise.

Below right:
probably the world's best-known lager.

INTO VESTERBRO

Turn left down Vesterbrogade, and left again onto Colbjørnsensgade. You are now in the red-light area as you will surmise from the clubs and interesting window displays. Turn right into Istedgade and left down Helgoslandgade into Halmtørvet, a former cattle market and now home to several cafés. Opposite is **Øksnehallen** ❸ (Halmtørvet 11; tel: 33 86 04 00; charge for exhibitions), an old cattle market now regenerated into a large and lovely cultural space.

Continue down Halmtørvet and turn right six streets down into **Skydebanegade**. Walk past the yellow townhouses and cross the main road. Go through the gate in the imposing brick wall opposite, which leads into **Skydebanehaven**, a park that once belonged to the Royal Shooting Club (now the City Museum), one of the first buildings in Vesterbro, which was granted permission to be built in the 1750s and was inaugurated in 1786.

Walk through the kids' play area and follow the path to the exit. Take a left onto Vesterbrogade; the **City Museum** (Kobenhavns ByMuseet) is located on your left.

The City Museum

First, take a look outside the **City Museum** ❹ (Vesterbrogade 59; tel: 33 21 07 72; www.kbhbymuseum.dk; Wed 10am–9pm, Thur–Mon 10am–4pm; charge, under-17s free, Fri free). You can admire the model of 16th-century Copenhagen, which makes for some interesting comparisons with the city today. Inside, the museum takes you from Copenhagen's early days as a little fishing village to modern times,

Food and Drink 🍴

② LES TROIS COCHONS
Værnedamsvej 10; tel: 33 31 70 55; www.cofoco.dk; Mon–Sat noon–3pm, daily 5.30pm–midnight; €
This atmosperic, elegant old butcher's shop delivers both style and good food at a very good price.

③ THAI TAKEAWAY
Værnedamsvej 9; tel: 33 26 26 42; Tue–Sun 4–10pm; €
Lovely fresh, aromatic Thai food; the locals claim it is the best in town. Seating available for about eight.

④ BANG AND JENSEN
Istedgade 130; tel: 33 25 53 18; daily 8am–2pm; €
A former pharmacy, now a cool and very popular café. Particularly good brunches.

⑤ ROCCOS
Istedgade 119; tel: 31 21 04 40; daily 9am–11pm; €
Tiny coffee house that does excellent coffee.

using some atmospheric reconstructions as well as fascinating objects from the collection.

Værnedamsvej

Back on Vesterbrogade, turn left and continue to the junction with Frederiksberg Allé. Then, turn right up **Værnedamsvej ❺**, famous for its gourmet shopping and a good place for lunch or early supper; try **Les Trois Cochons**, see ⑪②, or for a later meal or takeaway, the **Thai Takeaway**, see ⑪③, is excellent. Even if you are not going to eat, check out the street anyway, not least for chocolate shop **Summerbird** at No. 9.

Come back down onto Vesterbrogade and then cross the road into Oehlenschlægersgade where you will find, on the corner with Kaalundsgade, an extraordinary mosaic-covered bar, **Art and Colour ❻** (Wed–Thur 7pm–midnight, Fri–Sat 7pm–2am) – reminiscent of Gaudi's work in Barcelona – all lovingly put together by the late Nigerian-born artist Manuel Tafat.

The Carlsberg Brewery

Continue down to Istedgade and turn right. Continue past four or five streets. If you want a bite to eat, there are several good cafés along here, notably **Bang and Jensen**, see ⑪④, as well as some interesting independent shops. Cross the road and turn left onto Enghavevej, passing **Roccos**, see ⑪⑤, on your left. Keep going and turn right at quite a large crossroads onto cobbled Ny Carlsberg Vej, where

you are heading for the **Carlsberg Brewery ❼** (Carlsberg Bryggerierne).

You can see an archway from the end of the road. As you get there, look to your left to see the tall **winding chimney** decorated with lotus flowers (hard to see from a distance) and gargoyles (copied from Notre-Dame in Paris). Carlsberg want to prove that an industrial chimney could be beautiful so commissioned one of Copenhagen's most celebrated architects, Vilhelm Dahlerup, to design this one in 1900.

The first archway, called the **Dipylon Tower**, was built in 1892 and originally housed two malting floors; malt was loaded in and out of carriages through tubes in the gate's ceiling. The

Above from far left: performance in front of Øsknehallen; retro Carlsberg posters; inside the Carlsberg Brewery.

Above: a bear in a beer.

Carlsberg Beer

The Carlsberg brewery was set up by ale-brewer Jacob Christian Jacobsen (1811–87) in 1847, the year that he produced his first commercial beer using the new German lagering process. He named the brewery after his five-year old son Carl (1842–1914); 'berg' refers to the hill on which it was built. Carl built a second brewery close by in 1881 and took the swastika, an ancient sacred symbol found in a number of civilizations including Greece and Rome, as the new Carlsberg trademark. Both father and son espoused perfection, Jacobsen *père* even citing it in his will, 'In working the brewery it should be a constant purpose, regardless of immediate gain, to develop the art of making beer to the greatest possible degree of perfection'.

Above: the famous elephants mark the entrance to the old brewery.

Getting Home
If you don't want to walk all the way home, walk down Rahbeks Allé away from Pile Allé, to Vesterbrogade, where you can pick up the 6A bus back into town.

figure group on the roof, by sculptor Stephen Sinding, is called *The Bell Strikers*. The mosaics on the other side of the gate show Carl Jacobsen, his wife Ottilia and son and heir Alf (who died in 1890); Vilhelm Dahlerup and master builder S.P. Beckmann; and, representing the brewery's employees, office manager Christian Grønlund, Professor R. Hesberg, Chief Inspector V. Henningsen and an ordinary brewery worker.

Go through and you will see another archway held up by the four, famous lifesize **Carlsberg elephants**, designed in 1901, also by Dahlerup. These were partly inspired by the elephants holding up the organ in Our Saviour's Church (Vor Frelsers Kirke, *see p.84*) and partly by Bernini's obelisk-carrying elephant in Piazza Minerva in Rome. Note the copper busts of Carl and Ottilia Jacobsen looking down from a gallery at the top of the gate.

The Renaissance-style building on the right of the gate is the **Brew House**, with a balcony modelled on those in the Palazzo Bavilaque in Verona. On the roof is a large copper sculpture representing *Thor's Battle Against the Giants*, proposed by C.J. Bonnesen for the fountain at Langelinie, though the final design was Anders Bundgaard's *Gefion* group (*see p.51*). Carl asked the sculptor for a copy to ornament the Brew House.

Right: The Carlsberg Visitor Centre has 13,000 of its 16,000 Carlsberg label and bottle designs on display.

Walk under the 'Elephant Gate' to the end, passing, on your left, the **Carlsberg Museum** (Valby Langgade 1; tel: 33 27 12 73; www.visitcarlsberg.dk; Mon–Fri 10am–3pm; free), which tells the story of the Jacobsen family and the Carlsberg Foundation. Turn left onto Valby Langgade and then take the first left into Gamle Carlsberg Vej, where about half way down on the left you will find the **Carlsberg Visitor Centre**.

The Carlsberg Visitor Centre

The **Carlsberg Visitor Centre** ❽ (Carlsberg Besøgscenter; Gamle Carlsberg Vej 11; tel: 33 27 13 14/12 82; www.visitcarlsberg.dk; Tue–Sun 10am–4pm; charge) is in listed buildings that belonged to the first brewery; they date from 1867 when they were rebuilt following a fire. The exhibition offers interesting insight into brewing past and present, using light, sound, smells and interactive media. You can also view a collection of Carlsberg label and bottle designs, see the dray horses in their stables and, of course, sample (for free) a beer (or soft drink) in a very airy, attrac-tive bar, dominated by the great copper kettles that are used to brew Carlsberg's special beers.

If you have time to visit the **Bakke-huset**, the oldest building in the area, dating from the 1650s when it was an inn on the road to Copenhagen, retrace your steps to the top of Ny Carlsberg Vej and continue down Pile Allé. Take the first right and the museum is on the right-hand side.

Bakkehuset

From 1787, the **Bakkehuset** ❾ (Rahbeks Allé 23, tel: 33 31 43 62; www.bakkehusmuseet.dk; Wed–Thur, Fri–Sat 11am–3pm; charge), was home to Kamma and Lyhne Rahbek, literary personalities of the 19th-century Golden Age *(see p.59)*. It is now a cultural museum, furnished in the style of 1802–30. The poets Johannes Ewald (1743–81) and Adam Oehlenschläger (1779–1850, *see box and p.70*), are featured heavily (Oehlenschläger was the Rahbeks' son-in-law) and there is also memorablilia relating to Hans Christian Andersen (1805–75, *see p.56*), who came here often in his youth.

Nordic Romance

Born in Vesterbro, Adam Oehlenschläger was the pioneer of Romantic poetry and drama in Denmark. He was first inspired in 1802 after a 16-hour conversation with the Danish philosopher Henrik Steffens, who was causing a sensation lecturing on the hitherto unknown 'modern' German poets Goethe and Schiller. By the age of 26, Oehlenschläger was universally recognised as Denmark's leading poet. He is also the author of Denmark's national anthem, 'Der er et Yndigt Land' ('There is a Lovely Country').

THE OLD INNER CITY

This circular walk takes you through the oldest part of Copenhagen and encompasses Strøget, Copenhagen's long 'walking street', Gammel Strand (Old Beach) and the University or Latin Quarter. It is now a very lively area full of shops, bars and restaurants.

> **DISTANCE** 3.5km (2 miles)
> **TIME** A half/full day
> **START/END** Rådhuspladsen
> **POINTS TO NOTE**
> This walk takes quite a while if you visit everything. However, if you want to combine part of it with other walks, from Højbro Plads you can visit Slotsholmen *(see p.76)* or continue down Strøget to Kongens Nytorv and Nyhavn *(see pp.43–6)*.

Above from top:
taking a leisurely walk on Strøget; the Caritas Fountain.

Look Up
Oddly enough, it can be easy to miss the architecture on Strøget, so much is going on at eye-level. But don't forget to look up to see the variety of styles and decorations in this ancient, if relatively newly built, quarter.

With the exception of Slotsholmen *(see p.76)*, this is the oldest part of Copenhagen. Predominantly built in wood, the old city was a martyr to fire and almost completely demolished in 1728 and 1795. The first fire destroyed nearly 50 per cent of the medieval city and made 20 per cent of the population homeless; the second pretty much finished off the job. So, although the area has been inhabited for over 700 years, there are very few buildings that remain from before the 18th century.

Start at Rådhuspladsen *(see p.74)*, which was built in the 19th century just inside the old city walls (now demolished) and walk down Frederiksberggade, one of the five streets that make up **Strøget**, (literally 'stripe' and pronounced 'stroll'), which forms an uninterrupted link with royal Kongens Nytorv *(see p.43)* by the harbour.

This western end of Strøget is the least sophisticated part, characterised by fast-food joints and cheap fashion stores, in contrast with the middle and final stretches, where you will find Danish design and top fashion brands.

GAMMELTORV

Follow the cobbles to the first large open area that you come to. This is the site of Havn, Copenhagen's oldest village. **Gammeltorv** ❶ (Old Square), on your left, is the city's oldest meeting place where, in the Middle Ages, everything took place; a little like Rådhuspladsen today.

Gammeltorv suffered in both fires and the town hall that had stood facing inwards on what is now the intersection with **Nytorv** ❷ (New Square), was burnt down on both occasions. Rebuilt in the same place after 1728, after the second fire it was rebuilt on Nytorv *(see opposite)*, in the hope that the space created would act as a windbreak in the event of another fire. You can see its old outline in pale stone where the fruit-and-vegetable market usually stands.

On your left, you will see the **Caritas Fountain** (Springvandet). This is Copenhagen's oldest external water supply and is linked by pipes to a water source 6km (4 miles) away. It was a gift to the city in 1608 from Christian IV and the pregnant woman and two children represent *Caritas* (Charity), and symbolise the king's love for his people. The water flows from her breasts and the small boy taking a pee.

Behind the fountain, have a look at **Nos 10** and **14**. If it is open, inside the gate of No. 14 is a relief depicting the history of the square and No. 10, now a Chinese restaurant, was once the site of the village pond. A plaque commemorates the original town of Havn.

The curved façade of **Café Stelling**, designed by Arne Jacobsen (who also designed the Radisson SAS Royal Hotel *(see p.27)*, stands nearby on the corner of Skindergade.

NYTORV

On your right is where the gallows and whipping post used to stand on Nytorv. Branding and whipping took place until the late 1780s. The outline of the paler stones on Nytorv shows the position of the whipping post.

On the right-hand side, on the former site of the Royal Orphanage, which burnt down in the fire of 1728, you will find the classical porticoed grandeur of the **Domhuset**, the third town hall. This was built by the architect C.F. Hansen between 1805–15 (with a delay in 1807 when the British bombarded the city); Hansen was also responsible for rebuilding the cathedral, Church of Our Lady

Above from far left: inside Café Stelling; fashionable Strøget; the old city rooftops.

Gallows on Nytorv
Executions at the gallows on Nytorv were well attended by the locals and, shockingly, for many were a form of entertainment. Between 1720 and 1730 there were 14 executions; sadly, most of them impoverished women driven to killing their newborn babies. The last execution, of two counterfeiters, took place in 1758.

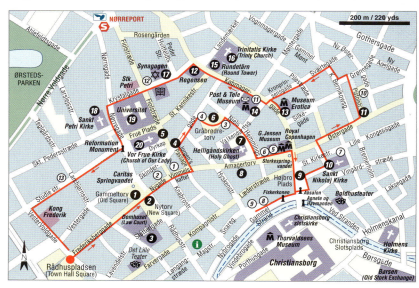

The Bells Toll
At 8pm on Thursday 20 October, just before the 1728 fire took hold of Helligåndskirken, its carillon bells, which rang out every half hour, played 'Turn your anger, Lord, by mercy'.

Below right: fountain in Gråbrødretorv.

(see p.42). The Domhuset was the town hall until 1905 when, owing to space issues, a new one was built on Rådhuspladsen (Town Hall Square). It is still used as Copenhagen's main Law Court and is the largest in Denmark. On its far side, on **Slutterigade ③** (Prison Street), you can see the two enclosed bridges (one of which is the 'Bridge of Sighs') that linked the courthouse to the prison, which was built in 1813–16.

INTO THE LATIN QUARTER

Carry on down Strøget until you reach the crossroads of Knabroestræde and Skoubogade – take a left for chocolate heaven at **PB Chokolade**, see ⑪①, or

La Glace, see ⑪②. Otherwise, continue until you see a sign for **Jorgen's Passage ④** on your left, an appealing arcade with some good kids' and home decor shops. Walk through to the end. Opposite is **Fiolstræde ⑤** – in the centre of the Latin Quarter around the university – with a few pretty outdoor restaurants, the back of the Church of Our Lady (Vor Frue Kirke), and some good antiquarian/second-hand bookshops at Nos 24 and 34–36, both with an English selection of books.

Gråbrødretorv

Turn right down Skindergade (Hide Street), originally home to furriers and tanners, and walk through to **Gråbrø-**

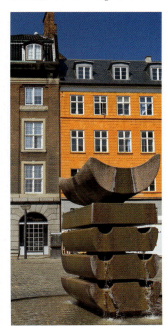

Food and Drink

① PB CHOKOLADE
Skoubogade 1; tel: 33 93 07 17; €€€
Not cheap but delicious. Specialities include delicacies filled with cream, fruit, nuts, truffle, spices and alcohol.

② LA GLACE
Skoubogade 3–5; tel: 33 14 46 46; www.laglace.dk; Mon–Thur 8.30am–5.30pm, Fri 8.30am–6pm, Sat 9am– 5pm, Sun (Sept–Mar) 11am–5pm (serving stops 30 mins earlier); €€
This traditional cake shop/café dating from 1870 is a Copenhagen institution. They make cakes for the queen so they must be good!

③ PEDER OXE
Gråbrødretorv 11; tel: 33 11 00 77; www.pederoxe.dk; 11am–1am; €€
Offers everything from a light lunch, tradtional sandwich or salad bar to full three-course meal. Emphasis on fresh organic produce. Friendly and based in an 18th-century building.

④ SPORVEJEN
Grabrødretorv 17; tel: 33 13 31 01; Mon–Sat 11am–midnight, Sun noon–midnight; €
Cheap and cheerful fare (omelettes, burgers etc) in an old Copenhagen tram. Sit out on the square in summer.

dretorv ⑥ (Grey Brothers Square), named after the grey-clad monks who lived here from 1238 in Copenhagen's first monastery. The monks were turned out just before the Reformation in 1536, and the monastery became a hospital. Many of the houses here date from after the fire of 1728 and are known as 'fire houses', a gabled, brick-built design that was introduced in the hope that it would be more fire-safe than the medieval timbered buildings that burnt so easily.

The second fire of 1795 destroyed much of the rebuild – the style that followed was plainer and more classical. The square is now filled with restaurants and is a pleasant place to eat out in summer. **Peder Oxe**, see ⑪③, or **Sporvejen**, see ⑪④, are good options if you are already thinking about lunch.

Church of the Holy Ghost

Cross the square and then take a right onto Niels Hemmingsgade. The church here is the **Church of the Holy Ghost** ⑦ (Helligåndskirken; Niels Hemmingsensgade 5; tel: 33 37 65 40; www.helligaandskirken.dk; Mon–Fri noon–4pm; music and prayers Mon–Fri noon except Jul–Aug; Sunday service 10am).

A hospice stood on this site as early as 1296. It was incorporated into the monastery in 1474. Most of the church, including the bells that were given by Christian IV in 1647, was destroyed in 1728. Even the coffins under the floor were destroyed. What survived the fire – the **Helligåndshuset**

(now used for markets and exhibitions); **Christian IV's baroque portal**, the main door, made in 1630 and originally intended for the Stock Exchange *(see p.77)*; and **Griffenfeld's Chapel** (the round burial chapel on the north side) – constitute some of the oldest architectural remains in Copenhagen. The church was reopened in 1732. Admirers of the philosopher Søren Kirkegaard might like to note that it was here that he first saw Régine, the girl to whom he became engaged, but whom he subsequently rejected.

Architecture after 1728

After 1728, there were attempts to reduce the city's vulnerability to fire, including a ban on half-timbered houses. A design for narrow 'fire houses', two or three storeys high, with a wide gable, typically with two or three windows and a small oval window at the top, was also introduced. A few of these remain but much of the rebuild was still done in wood as it was cheaper than brick. But after 1795, the construction of houses in brick was enforced, and terraces had to have oblique corners to enable fire engines to get around more easily, thus creating small octagonal squares all over the city. The style also changed and a new, neoclassical style, inspired by ancient Greece and Rome, without balconies, bays or any unnecessary ornament, was introduced.

Modern 17th-Century Design

Formerly the modern town house of a wealthy 17th-century merchant, Amagertorv 6 still sees the rich passing through its portals to buy beautiful porcelain from Royal Copenhagen.

Below right: time for a break.

AMAGERTORV

Turn left out of the church back onto Strøget and you are almost immediately on **Amagertorv ❽**, another square punctuating the 1.5-km (1-mile) length of Strøget. From here on, the shopping on Strøget becomes infinitely smarter.

Georg Jensen, Royal Copenhagen and Stork Fountain

To your left you will find two great Danish design institutions, the silver-smith **Georg Jensen** (Amagertorv 4; tel: 33 14 02 29; Mon–Thur 10am–6pm, Fri 10am–7pm, free) and **Royal Copenhagen** (Amagertorv 6; tel: 38 14 92 97; www.royalcopenhagen.com Mon–Fri 10am–5.30pm, Sat 9am–2pm; free), the 17th-century, hand-painted porcelain manufacturer. Housed side by side in two ornate, rather lovely Renaissance buildings, both have free museums – Georg Jensen in the basement and Royal Copenhagen on the second floor, where, with an appointment made a few days in advance (tel: 38 14 96 97, rctourism@royalcopenhagen.com), you can paint your own traditional 'Blue Floral' design on a blown-out egg (150dkk, approx 30 mins) or a porcelain plate (250dkk, approx 45 mins), under the eye of a professional Royal Copenhagen artist.

Next door is **Illums Bolighus**, a furniture design mecca *(see p.18)* and

---

Food and Drink 🍴

⑤ ILLUMS BOLIGHUS
Amagertorv 10; tel: 33 14 19 41; Mon–Fri 10am–7pm, Sat 10am–5pm; €
Light, airy, top-floor café with balcony, family area and good coffee.

⑥ THE ROYAL CAFE
Amagertorv 6; tel: 38 14 95 27; www.royalcafe.dk; daily during shopping hours; €–€€
Café with courtyard set in a Renaissance building. All dishes are served on Royal Copenhagen porcelain. Speciality of 'smushi' – sushi-inspired smørrebrød.

⑦ CAFEEN I NIKOLAJ
Nikolaj Plads 10; tel: 33 11 63 13; Mon–Sat 11.30am–5pm; €–€€
Traditional food, well presented in a delightful church restaurant/café. Eat outside on the cobbles in summer.

⑧ THORVALDSENS HUS
Gammel Strand 34; tel: 33 32 04 00; daily 11am–midnight; €–€€€€
French-inspired restaurant with courtyard serving good food and great Sunday brunch. Gourmet menu excellent value at 325dkk.

⑨ KROGS FISKERESTAURANT
Gammel Strand 38; tel: 33 15 89 15; www.krogs.dk; Mon–Sat 5.30pm–midnight; €€€€
Booking is essential if you wish to dine at Copenhagen's oldest and most expensive fish restaurant. The elegant interior dates from 1910, the fixed menu starts at 750dkk.

ahead of you, the **Stork Fountain**, Storkespringvandet (though the birds are actually herons), which was erected in 1894 to mark the silver wedding of Crown Prince Frederik (VIII) and his wife, Princess Louise. It is now a popular meeting place.

If you are in need of a drink or a bite to eat, three good places spring to mind: the café at the top of **Illums**, see ⑪⑤, the powder-puff-pink **Royal Café**, see ⑪⑥, or the charming **Cafeen i Nikolaj**, a short walk away at the Church of St Nicholas (see ⑪⑦ and below).

HØJBRO PLADS

From here, turn right into **Højbro Plads ❾**, home to a dramatic equestrian statue of Copenhagen's founder, Bishop Absalon. It dates from 1902 and is the work of Danish sculptors Vilhelm Bissen, who cast the figure, and Martin Nyrop, who was responsible for the plinth. Walk down and, to your right, you will find **Gammel Strand** (Old Beach) where, from early days, fishermen used to bring in their herring catches and their wives (the 'fishwives') sold them. **Fiskerkonen**, a statue of a sturdy fishwife by Christian Svejstrup Madsen, dates from 1940 and stands on the corner of the steps down to the canal that still separates the Old Town from Slotsholmen *(see p.76)*. In 1940 there was still a regular fish market here.

If you are hungry for a solid, proper, delicious lunch, there are several very good fish restaurants along Gammel Strand, including **Thorvaldsens Hus**,

see ⑪⑧, and **Krogs Fiskerestaurant**, see ⑪⑨. On the other side of the canal, the porticoed building behind the Fishwife is the castle church, **Christiansborg Slotskirke** *(see p.78)* and to the right of that, the ochre building is the **Thorvaldsen Museum** *(see p.78)*. Looking ahead from the statue of Absalon, the copper roofs and twisting spire belong to the Renaissance **Børsen**, the old Stock Exchange *(see p.77)*. The spire to the right is **Holmens Kirke**, the old navy church *(see p.76)*.

Above from far left: street café on Højbro Plads; modern glassware; the Royal Café; Bishop Absalon.

Above: porcelain cat from the Royal Copenhagen museum.

Royal Copenhagen

Royal Copenhagen, the Danish manufacturer of hand-made and hand-painted porcelain, was founded in 1775 by Franz Müller, a chemist who had succeeded in mastering the difficult art of Chinese-style hard-paste porcelain. Its first designs – 'Blue Fluted', dating from 1775, based on Chinese floral motifs and 'Blue Flower', which is a little more naturalistic and dates from 1779 – were in cobalt blue, the only colour to withstand the high firing temperatures required. Its most ambitious design, 'Flora Danica', shows copies of botanical drawings and was originally commissioned by the king for Catherine the Great in 1790. The 1,802 pieces in the range took 12 years for one artist to paint. All three designs are still in production today.

Above: exhibit at the Post & Tele Museum; a painting from the Erotica Museum.

Before turning back, cross to the middle of the bridge and look over the left side down to the water where you will see eight figures with their hands outstretched pleadingly beneath the surface. This little-known figure group depicts part of the legend of **Agnete and the Merman**, a story in which peasant girl Agnete marries a merman and has seven sons but then fails to return after visiting her home village. The sculpture is the work of sculptor Suste Bonnén and was placed here in 1992.

CHURCH OF ST NICHOLAS

Walk back up towards Strøget and take a right down Lille Kirkestræde to the **Church of St Nicholas** ❿ (Sankt Nikolaj Kirke; Nikolaj Plads 10; tel: 33 18 17 80; www.kunsthallen nikolaj.dk), named after the patron saint of sailors – an apt sponsor in a

seaboard town. The mother church of the Reformation in 1536, it survived the 1728 fire, but was not so lucky in 1795 when everything but the tower was razed to the ground. Rebuilt in rather imposing red brick in the early 20th century, it is now an exhibition hall for modern art.

ON TO KØBMAGERGADE

Cross over Store Kirkestraede back onto Strøget. Turn right down to Kristen Bernikows Gade and cross the road (to your right you will see the back of Magasin du Nord *(see p.43)* and a small flower market. Continue until you reach a sign-posted archway for **Pistolstræde** ⓫. Walk to the end, past various smart shops, until you reach the little courtyard with **L'Alsace**, see Ⓨ❿ (which has hosted Pope John Paul II and Elton John no less), where you will

(see p.43)

My Generation

The muscular figure group on Gammel Strand, 'Slægt Løfter Slægt' (Generation Raises Generation) is by the expressionist painter Svend Wiig Hansen (1922–97). It was erected in 2000 in memory of the Minister of Culture Julius Bomholt.

Right: love is in the air.

Food and Drink 🍴

❿ L'ALSACE
Ny Østergade 9; tel:33 14 57 43; www.alsace.dk; Mon–Sat 11.30am–midnight; €–€€€€
Gourmet food from Continental Europe, specialising in Alsace, in attractive surroundings. A three-course lunch menu at 245dkk is good value.

⓫ CAFE HOVEDTELEGRAFEN
Købmagergade 37; tel: 33 41 09 86; www.cafehovedtelgrafen.dk; Mon–Sat 10am–5pm, Sun noon–4pm, kitchen shuts an hour earlier; €
This rooftop café offers an airy interior and an outdoor terrace over looking the rooftops of the old town. Snacks and main meals (mainly fish) are good.

see the timbered backs of 17th-century houses; unusual in an Old Town that has succumbed to two major fires.

Walk through to Grønnegade, a pretty street (look at the houses to your right) and turn left, then right back on to Kristen Bernikows Gade. Take the first left on to Sværtergade. This turns into Kronprinsensgade, one of Copenhagen's poshest shopping streets (even if it does have a 7/11 on the corner). **Summerbird Chocolaterie** (Kronprincensgade 11; tel: 33 93 80 40), another well-known chocolate maker, can be found along here.

At the end you reach Købmagergade. For the **Museum Erotica**, turn left towards Amagertorv, otherwise turn right. Opposite you is the **Post & Tele Museum** and further down on your right, the **Round Tower; Trinity Church** next to it; and, opposite, **Regensen ⑫**, a 17th-century student hall of residence, which is still in use.

Museum Erotica

The appeal of the **Museum Erotica ⑬** (Købmagergade 24; tel: 33 12 03 46; www.museumerotica.dk; May–Sept: daily 10am–11pm, Oct–Apr: Sun–Thur 10am–8pm, Fri–Sat 10am–10pm; charge) is a matter of taste. The ground floor offers plenty of depictions of the human form in art over the centuries; the second floor offers some interesting social history relating to prostitutes in Copenhagen in the 19th century as well as a section on the love lives of Hollywood stars of the 1930s–60s, especially Marilyn Monroe. The first floor has displays relating to the modern sex industry and unorthodox sex; some of it is particularly unedifying.

Post & Tele Museum

Copenhagen's main post office is home to the **Post & Tele Museum ⑭** (Købmagergade 37; tel: 33 41 09 00; Tue, Thur–Sat 10am–5pm, Wed 10am–8pm, Sun noon–4pm; free), which charts the history of communication from the 17th century. Even though labelling is mostly in Danish, it makes for an interesting browse. Ignore the stamp collection and head up to **Café Hovedtelegrafen** for excellent views, see ⑪⑪.

Above from far left: folk musicians; Marilyn Monroe display inside the Museum Erotica.

Streets off Strøget

Although this walk takes in the major sights, don't be afraid to wander down streets that take your fancy; there are many treasures (historical and retail) around almost every corner. Unexpected finds are part of the pleasure of ambling around this area North and south of Strøget, the streets offer more individual shopping in little one-off boutiques, record and second-hand shops. Streets to head for include Skindergade, Larsbjørnstræde and the three parralel streets: Vestergade, Studiestræde, Sankt Peders Stræde; and Læderstræde and Kompagnistræde, which run into each other; the latter is especially good for antiques shops.

Russian Riding
In 1715, Tsar Peter of
Russia rode his horse
to the top of the
209-m (686-ft) ramp
inside the Round
Tower, followed by his
wife in a carriage. Now
there are yearly uni-
cycle races to the top.

Below: spa at First
Hotel Sankt Petri.

Round Tower

Continue down Købmagergade until
you see the **Round Tower** (Rundetårn)
⑮ (Kobmagergade 52a; tel: 33 73 03
73; www.rundetaarn.dk; Sept–May:
Mon–Sat 10am–5pm, Sun noon–5pm;
Jun–Aug: Mon–Sat 10am–8pm, Sun
noon–8pm; charge), the round red-
brick tower on your right. This unusual
building is a 17th-century observatory,
built by Christian IV and thought to
be mentioned in H.C. Andersen's
fairytale of the *Soldier and the Tinder
Box* where a dog is described as having
'eyes as big as a tower'.

Andersen knew this tower well and,
as an observatory, it was literally an

'eye' on the heavens. Inside, there is a
wide cobbled ramp, designed for a
horse and cart to use; the only practical way of taking heavy equipment all
the way to the top. There is also an art
gallery, formerly the university library,
about half way up.

Trinity Church

Next door is **Trinity Church** **⑯**
(Trinitatis Kirke; Købmagergade 52a/
Landemærket 12; tel: 33 37 65 40;
www.trinitatiskirke.dk; Mon–Sat
9.30am–4.30pm), commisioned as the
university church by Christian IV and
finished in 1657 under Frederik III.

Although the Round Tower survived
the blaze of 1728, the church suffered.
Its roof and the university library that
lay beneath it were charred to a crisp
and its interior damaged. But it
was quickly restored by 1731 and is now
a lovely white-and-gold Rococo affair
with a splendid Baroque altarpiece, a
three-faced Rococo clock, a vaulted roof
picked out in gold, galleries running
down both side walls and a fabulous
gold- and silver-coloured organ. If it is
open, it is worth a visit; otherwise, look
down the nave through a glass panel
as you start up the Round Tower.

KRYSTALGADE

Continue and turn left up Krystalgade,
the spire of the Church of Our Lady
(Vor Frue Kirke) in view. The large
red-brick building a little way up on
your right is Copenhagen's **Grand
Synagogue** **⑰** (Synagogen; usually
closed to the public). The centre for

Judaism in Denmark, it dates from 1883 and, amazingly, survived the Nazi occupation. Its interior is notable for Egyptian-influenced elements. Its sacred Torah scrolls were hidden in Trinity Church during World War II.

Cross over Filostræde. The back of the university building is on your left (you can see the book stacks through the windows) and the **First Hotel Sankt Petri**, see ⑪⑫, where you can settle down for an early evening cocktail, is a little further up on your right.

NØRREGADE

At the end of the street, at the smart designer furniture shop R.O.O.M., take a left onto Nørregade. On your right is the **Church of St Peter** ⑱.

Church of St Peter
The first Church of St Peter (Sankt Petri Kirke; Larslejsstæde 11; tel: 33 13 38 33; Mar–Nov: Tue–Sun 11am–3pm) was built here in 1386 in the Romanesque style. It burnt down and was replaced, *c.*1450, with a Gothic structure, minus the transepts, which were added in the 17th century.

During the Reformation, the church was deconsecrated and turned into a canon foundry, but in 1585 it was reinstated and given to the German-speaking population by Frederik II. German was the main language spoken by the court and, as a result, Sankt Petri became an important intellectual, economic and political meeting place.

The fire of 1728 destroyed its interior, and new decoration, including the Baroque main entrance (1730s) and the copper-clad spire (1757), were introduced. Its vaulted sepulchral chapel (1681–83), which has some impressive

Food and Drink 🍴

⑫ **BAR ROUGE: FIRST HOTEL SANKT PETRI**
Krystalgade 22; tel: 33 45 91 00; www.hotelsktpetri.com; Sun–Thur 4pm–1am, Fri–Sat 4pm–2am; €€€
Voted best Danish hotel in 2006, Bar Rouge is the nicest of the bars in Hotel Sankt Petri bars. It is to the right at the top of the escalators. There is also a rather dark though stylish café on the ground floor.

Royal Weddings

When Crown Prince Frederik married Australian commoner Mary Donaldson in May 2004, walking her down the aisle of the Church of Our Lady (Vor Frue Kirke), he was following in the footsteps of some of his forebears: Queen Margrethe I who, at the age of nine, married the Norwegian king Haakan in 1363; and Christian I who married his queen, Dorothea, here in 1449. The Danish monarchy holds the record for unbroken succession from the Viking chief Gorm the Old, father of Harald Bluetooth, who died in 959, of fifty kings (predominantly named Frederik or Christian) and two queens, both Margrethe – the second currently on the throne.

The Bells of St Mary's

Of the four bells
belonging to the
Church of Our Lady,
one dates from 1490
(although it is not
original to the church)
and another one,
'Stormklokken',
weighs 4 tons and
is the heaviest bell
in the country.

Below: the light and
bright interior of the
Church of Our Lady.

statuary, is the resting place of the Rococo, royal architect Nicolai Eigtved (1701–54).

The University

On your left, as you walk towards the Church of Our Lady, there is a square. The building facing the side of the church is the **University ⑲** (Universitet). There has been a university in Copenhagen since 1479. It was located on the corner of Nørregade and Studiestræde until the Reformation in 1536, when it was moved across the street to the vacated Bishops Palace.

The fires of 1728 and 1795 made short work of any ancient buildings and the current one dates from the 19th century. The portrait busts are of illustrious professors.

Church of Our Lady

There has been a church on the site of the cathedral, the **Church of Our Lady ⑳** (Vor Frue Kirke; Nørregade, Vor Frue Plads, tel: 33 37 65 40; daily 8am–5pm), since the 12th century. What the fires of 1728 and 1795 left intact, the British bombardment of 1807 destroyed when the navy used the church spire as a target. The current building, designed by C.F. Hansen, dates from 1829 and only the tower and the walls of the side aisles remain of the medieval building. Of particular note are the reliefs and imposing marble statues by Bertel Thorvaldsen *(see p.78)* of **Christ and the 12 Apostles** (with Judas replaced by St Paul) dating from 1839; these are on the altar and along the side walls.

The statues outside are **King David** (1860) by L.A. Jerichat and **Moses** (1853) by H.W. Bissen. The **monument** opposite, which was erected in 143, commemorates the 400th anniversary of the Reformation.

Cross the road and head down Studiestræde opposite the Church of Our Lady, past **Robert's Café**, see ⑪⑬. Take a left at the end and walk down and you will be back on Rådhuspladsen.

THE HARBOUR AREA

This walk is a short but colourful one, starting in Kongens Nytorv (King's New Square), the height of 17th-century aristocratic elegance, and leading down to Nyhavn, the harbour, once populated by unseemly mariners and now an attractive and popular outdoor area with lots of restaurant and bars.

In the Middle Ages, Kongens Nytorv, an elegant square that now seems integral to Copenhagen, was outside the city walls and quite a way from the banks of the Sound. It began to develop under Frederik III (1648–70). In 1671–73, his son Christian V (1670–99) commissioned a canal (now called Nyhavn, or 'New Harbour') to be dug from the Sound to the square so that merchant ships could sail inland and unload their cargo more easily. He also ordered landowners with property bordering on the square to build grand mansions or to sell their land to someone who would.

DISTANCE 1km (½ mile)
TIME 1hr (plus boat trip 1hr)
START Hôtel d'Angleterre
END Nyhavn
POINTS TO NOTE
If you don't take a harbour cruise, this is a nice walk to do at the end of the day, ending on Nyhavn for a drink or dinner. If you walk up one of the side streets onto Sankt Annae Plads, it connects easily with the walk of the Royal District *(see p.47).*

Above: the front door of the Hôtel d'Angleterre; Magasin du Nord is the city's biggest department store.

KONGENS NYTORV

Standing at the bottom of **Strøget** *(see p.33)* you face Kongens Nytorv with Nyhavn opposite, at the bottom. To your left, at the corner of the square is Copenhagen's swankiest hotel, the **Hôtel d'Angleterre**; to your right on the opposite corner is **Magasin du Nord**, its oldest department store.

Hôtel d'Angleterre

The **Hôtel d'Angleterre** ❶ has seen its fair share of wealthy visitors since opening its doors in 1755. Guests have included H.C. Andersen, Grace Kelly, Winston Churchill, Margaret Thatcher, Bill Clinton, Woody Allen, Pierce Brosnan and Madonna. When Michael Jackson stayed in the 1980s, he was so enthralled by some of its furnishings that he wanted to buy them; when politely told they were not for sale, he offered to buy the entire hotel instead. Oddly enough, they declined.

Magasin du Nord

Originally a hotel, the **Magasin du Nord** ❷, dates from the 19th century. H.C. Anderson lived in its garret, when he lived at Vingårdstræde 6 in 1827, while he was studying for his exams at the age of 22. He wasn't very happy here. You can now visit his garret on the

Above from left:
the Charlottenborg
Palace gallery is the
venue for changing
exhibitions of contem-
porary Danish and
international art; pic-
turesque Nyhavn; the
crimson-and-gold
Royal Theatre.

**Hans Christian
Andersen**
Andersen always
loved the Royal
Theatre and liked
to live close by.
He wrote his first
fairytale, *The Tinder
Box*, in 1835 when he
lived at no. 20 (then
289) Nyhavn. He lived
at the Hôtel (now
Magasin) du Nord in
1838 and used to eat
his meals at Mini's,
now Café à Porta.

third floor (tel: 33 18 21 51; open during
shop hours; free). Magasin is also a good
stop for a coffee or bite to eat in an area
where you pay for the location.

The Royal Theatre and Charlottenborg Palace

The **Royal Theatre** ➌ (Det Kongelige
Teater; *see p.20*) stands opposite the
Magasin du Nord on the south side of
the square. There has been a theatre
here since 1748; the present theatre was
built in the 1870s, taking the classically
inspired Parisian Opera as its model.

To the east (have a look at the
mosaic ceiling of the archway as you
walk that way) is the **Charlottenborg
Palace** ➍ (Charlottenborgslot), built
between 1672 and 1783 by Frederik
III's illegitimate son Ulrik. It is an early
example of the Danish Baroque style.
Less than a century later, in 1754, it
became the Royal Academy of Fine
Arts, where painters, sculptors and
architects learned their trade. It is now
used for exhibitions.

Equestrian Statue of Christian V

Look to the centre of the square where
you will see a large **equestrian statue**
of **Christian V** ➎ dressed as a Roman
emperor, riding over the fallen figure
of Envy. The king is surrounded by
Queen Artemisia, Alexander the
Great, the goddess Pallas Athene and
Hercules. Sculpted by the Frenchman
Abraham César Lamoureux, it was the
first equestrian statue in Scandinavia
and was originally made of gilded lead
because bronze castings of this size
were not possible at the time. It has
been repaired many times and in 1946
was recast in bronze. The original can
now be found in Christian IV's Brewery
(Brygghus; *see p.80*).

NYHAVN

At the bottom of Kongens Nytorv lies
the 'New Harbour' or **Nyhavn** ➏,
lined with pastel-coloured, merchants'
houses that date from when the canal
was constructed. Their warehouses
stood at the end; a couple still survive
and are now smart, boutique hotels,
The Admiral and 71 Nyhavn *(see p.114)*.
The merchants could be close to their
precious cargoes, day and night.

But Nyhavn, with its attractive
wooden boats at anchor, is not just of

Food and Drink

① **CAP HORN**
Nyhavn 21; tel: 33 12 85 04;
www.caphorn.dk; daily 9am–1am
(lunch 11.30am–5pm; kitchen open
until 11pm); €€
Lunch at this cosy, appealing place
is usually Danish, while supper is
international. Dishes range from pasta
to duck, fresh lobster to fallow deer.

interest for its 18th-century mariners' past. From the 1880s, it was also the gateway to a new life in the US, since it was here that you bought your ticket from one of the many shipping offices that sprang up. A new start for many, although not for the 14 unfortunates who set sail to join the Titanic's maiden voyage in 1912 of whom only two survived.

The entrance to Nyhavn is heralded by a large **anchor**, honouring 1,600 Danish sailors who lost their lives in World War II. To the left as you face the Sound is the **Amber Museum** ❼ (Kongens Nytorv 2; tel: 33 11 67 00; www.houseofamber.com; Oct–Apr: daily 10am–5.30pm, May–Sept: daily 10am–7.30pm; charge) showcasing Denmark's national gemstone. When you learn that most amber deposits weigh 10g (½oz) or less each, you will understand the wonder of the chunk weighing a record-breaking 8.8kg (19lbs 6oz) that they have on display.

Nyhavn's North Side

This side of the canal is a popular restaurant area; sit inside or out (you will get blankets and heaters outside in winter) but grab a seat while you can, as it is almost always busy. The restaurants are all in old buildings and have names such as Skipperkroen (the Skipper's Inn), **Cap Horn**, see ⑪①, or Havruen (the Mermaid); they are linked to the lives and travels of the sailors who used to saunter along here looking for women, drink, a bed and possibly a fight.

Hans Christian Andersen used to live along here; at **Nos 18, 20** (both on the opposite side of the canal) and at **No 67**, two doors up from 71 Nyhavn.

Above: the equestrian statue of Christian V; artwork in front of the Charlottenborg Palace.

Ahoy Sailor!
Sailors have all but disappeared from Nyhavn. In the past, there was an average of 22,000 sailors from all over the world in the city at any one time, and it was not uncommon for ships to dock for two weeks. Nowadays ships often put in for less than a day.

Left: capturing the beauty of Nyhavn.

Above from far left: taking a boat trip on the Sound; toasting Copenhagen; a Royal Life Guard patrols Amalienborg; Sankt Annæ Plads at dusk.

Side Streets

The side streets off Nyhavn are well worth a look and, like the harbour itself, have come up in the world. The first turning on your left takes you up **Store Strandstræde** (Big Beach Street), the only remnant of its seafaring past is a tatoo parlour that claims to have been on the site since the 16th century.

There's a nice little restaurant called **Zeleste**, see ⑪②, along here – you'll recognise it by the kitsch, plastic crayfish hanging outside.

Continue along and at the end turn right, back on yourself, down **Lille Strandstræde** (Little Beach Street), also home to small galleries and designer clothes shops. If you are looking for a cheap sandwich, pop into **Thomas Sandwich Bar**, see ③. Carry on to the end and you will find yourself back on Nyhavn.

Boat Trip on the Sound

If you want to take a boat trip along the Sound, which is highly recommended, you will find the **DFDS** and **Netto Bådene** boats ❽, at the top of Nyhavn near the anchor. Netto Bådene is usually slightly cheaper. If you prefer a visit on land, get on a harbour bus at the end of Nyhavn for a similar ride along the Sound. Seeing the city from the water is restful and also helps you to better understand the layout of this waterside city, which began on the island of Slotsholmen.

On such a trip, you would expect to go up the Sound and pass by the new **Opera House** *(see p.86)*; **Langelinie**, **Kastellet** and *The Little Mermaid (see p.51)*; **Trekroner** (an 18th-century fort used once in 1801 against the British); back down along the **Christianshavn Kanal** *(see p.84)* and then down the **Frederiksberg Kanal**, past **Slotsholmen** *(see p.76)* and the royal palace, the **Brygghus**, the **Black Diamond** and **Holmens Kirke** before coming back to Nyhavn.

Food and Drink 🍴

② ZELESTE
Store Strandstraede 6; tel: 33 16 06 06; open daily 10am–1am; kitchen open 10.30am–10.30pm; www.zeleste.dk; €–€€

Pretty whitewashed restaurant with cobbled courtyard. Hearty menu changes regularly. Great brunches. Book to avoid disappointment.

③ THOMAS SANDWICH BAR
Lille Strandstræde 17; tel: 33 13 13 31; €

Tiny basement eatery with room for a handful of people. Makes excellent fresh savoury sandwiches.

THE ROYAL DISTRICT

This walk takes you through Copenhagen's grandest quarter, the Frederiksstad, and then by the sea along the banks of the Sound. A quiet spot now, except for tourists and people taking a stroll or riding bikes, this was once a heaving commercial and naval area.

In 1749, Frederik V laid the foundation stone for his building project, the Frederiksstad, a grand court district adorned with a large and beautiful church rivalling almost anything else in Europe. He was an absolute monarch, belonging to the 300-year-old Oldenburg dynasty and wanted to create something startling; and he did. He even got his wealthy subjects to pay for it.

The Amalienborg, a royal palace since 1794, was originally the home to several high-ranking ministers and was built on the site of Queen Sophie Amalie's palace, built in the 17th century, which burnt down during a theatrical performance for Christian V, on 19 April 1689.

Start at Sankt Annæ Plads **❶**. A large **equestrian statue of Christian X** (1912–1947) presides over the square. Walk down the right-hand side and you will pass the church and graveyard of the **Garrison's Church ❷** (Garnisons Kirke; free). This church was built to replace the castle chapel that had burnt down in 1689 *(see p.48)*. Copenhagen's garrison attended church here from 1706. The interior is dominated by two-storey galleries along the walls. The Baroque marble altarpiece dates from 1724.

> **DISTANCE** 4km (2½ miles)
> **TIME** A half day
> **START** Sankt Annæ Plads
> **END** Kongens Nytorv
> **POINTS TO NOTE**
> Most of the food options are towards the end of the walk near Bredgade, which makes this a good choice for a morning walk. Alternatively, have a picnic by the Sound or in Kastellet.

AMALIENBORG

From here, cross the square and turn left up **Amaliegade**. There are several embassies along here and the buildings are some of the most elegant and expensive in the city. If you need a bite to eat check out **Restaurant Amalie**, see ⓘ, or the equally popular **Café Toldboden**, see ②② *(see p.49)*. Go through the arch that leads into the

> ### Food and Drink 🍴
> **① RESTAURANT AMALIE**
> Amaliegade 11; tel: 33 12 88 10; opening hours; €€
> Charming, candle-lit, wood-panelled restaurant that serves up delicious Danish food. Good value for the quality. Book well ahead.

Above: Sankt Annæ Plads; one of the 14 Danish 'Fathers of the Church' outside the Marble Church.

Amaliegade Residents
Before he became a 'Prince of Denmark' in 1852, at the age of 34, Christian IX *(see p.49)* lived with his family in a yellow town house at Amaliegade 18. Four of his children were born there between 1843 and 1847.

Changing the Guard
The Amalienborg is guarded by the Royal Life Guards who do two-hour shifts. When the queen is in residence, they are replaced at noon by the guards from the Rosenborg Palace.

grandest part of the Frederiksstad, the square around which the four palaces of the **Amalienborg** ❸ stand.

The Palaces

The Amalienborg, a royal palace since 1794, was originally the home to several high-ranking ministers. It was built on the site of Queen Sophie Amalie's 17th-century palace, which burnt down during a theatrical performance on 19 April 1689.

The palaces were designed in the 1750s by the royal architect Nicolai Eigtved. The royal family moved in after a fire at Slotsholmen *(see p.76)*, and liked them so much that the king purchased all four. They have lived here ever since, members often occupying each palace at different times.

As you stand in the centre of the octagonal 'square' looking back at the colonnade, the palace to your right is **Christian VII's palace** ❹ (Christian VII's Palæ), one of the first to be finished before Eigtved died in 1754. This was originally the sumptuous home of Lord High Steward Adam Gottlob Moltke and the most expensive of the four; it is widely considered to be Denmark's best Rococo interior. Christian VII, who was schizophrenic, lived here from December 1794 until his death in 1808. The queen now uses it to welcome foreign dignitaries.

On the left of the colonnade, which connects the two palaces, you'll find **Christian IX's Palace** ❺ (Christian IX's Palæ), which is home to Queen Margrethe and Prince Henrik, and was originally known as Schack's Palace. Crown Prince Frederik VI and his wife Marie were the first Royals to move in and lived here for over 40 years. Frederik was Regent and ruled for his father from 1784–1808. Even so, he often needed his father's signature for affairs of state, so he had the colonnade built between the two

palaces, with a corridor running through it for easy access.

Turn your back on these palaces and the palace on your left is **Christian VIII's Palace** ❻ (Christian VIII's Palæ), originally called the Levetzau Palace. Part of the palace is open all year as a **museum** to the Glücksberg dynasty (tel: 33 12 21 86/08 08; www.amalien borgmuseet.dk; Nov–18 Dec and Jan–Apr: Tue–Sun 11am–4pm; May–Oct: daily 10am–4pm; guided tours in English, French, German and Danish; separate tours of the Bel-étage: every second week, Wed and Sun 11.30am, 1pm, 2.30pm; charge). Here, you can see the chintzy drawing room of Queen Louise and the studies of Frederik VIII, Frederik IX, Christian IX, and Christian X, which have all been moved from other parts of the Amalienborg.

On your right is **Frederik VIII's Palace** ❼ (Frederick VIII's Palæ), with a clock on its façade, which is the home of Crown Prince Frederik and his Australian wife, the Crown Princess Mary Donaldson.

In the centre of the square is an equestrian statue of **Frederik V**, dressed as a Roman emperor. Sculptor Jacques Saly took over 20 years to complete the statue owing, it is said, to his commitment to having fun, hence the delay. It was unveiled in 1771 with a 21-gun salute.

The Marble Church

You will see the spectacular **Marble Church** ❽ (Marmorkirken; Frederiksgade 4; tel: 33 15 01 44; www.marmorkirken.dk; Mon, Tue, Thur 10am–5pm; Wed 10am–6pm; Fri–Sun noon–5pm; free, but charge to climb dome) or, more properly, 'Frederikskirke' (after the monarch), if you stand with your back to the statue. It was designed as a very important part of the Frederiksstad by Nicolai Eigtved in 1740; yet, 30 years on, it remained unfinished and funds had run out. It

Food and Drink

② CAFE TOLDBODEN

Amaliegade 41; tel: 33 12 94 67; Mon–Fri 11am–4pm; €€€
Join the local suits who stop for their lunchtime *smørrebrød* in this 18th-century town house. Book to be sure of a seat.

Father-in-Law of Europe

Christian IX (1863–1906), for whom one of the Amalienborg palaces is named, came to be known as the 'father-in-law of Europe' because his six children married into the royal families of Sweden, Britain, Russia, Germany and France. A nephew of the childless Frederik VII (1848–63), he was the first king since Christian I (1448–81) not to succeed his father or grandfather, and, although a choice favoured by the Danes, he was not the nearest legal heir. Christian improved his claim by marrying Louise of Hesse, who was more closely related on the female side. His daughter Alexandra married King Edward VII of Britain (who reigned 1901–10), son of Queen Victoria.

In 1902, the beer baron Carl Jacobsen and his wife Ottilia set up the Carlsberg Foundation to promote Danish art and artists. Several of the statues along the Sound were commissioned by the foundation and date from 1909.

languished in ruins for over a century when help came in the guise of an industrialist, Carl Frederik Tietgenitz, and it was inaugurated in August 1894. A massive dome stands on 12 pillars and is covered in paintings of the 12 apostles, light flooding in from 12 skylights. At 31m (101ft) in diameter, the dome is second only in size to that of St Peter's in Rome, which measures 42m (137ft). You can go up at 3pm daily for some wonderful views.

Outside, at ground level, there are 14 Danish 'Fathers of the Church' and higher up, 18 figures of prophets, apostles and figures from Church history, finishing with Martin Luther.

Alexandr Nevsky Church

Coming out of the church, look to your left up Bredgade (an exclusive street full of antique shops and auction houses): you will see the golden onion domes of **Alexandr Nevsky Church** ❾ (Alexandr Nevsky Kirke; Bredgade 53; tel: 20 76 16 47 for group visits; Wed 11.30am–1.30pm), a Russian orthodox church, built in 1883 as a gift from Tsar Alexander III to mark his marriage to Princess Marie Dagmar.

Walk back to the Amalienborg and through the square to the Sound, where you will find **Amalie Haven** ❿, a pretty park directly across from the **Opera House** *(see p.86)*.

Marie Dagmar

Marie Dagmar, the second daughter of Christian IX, married the future Tsar Alexander III in St Petersburg in 1866. She had, in fact, been betrothed to Alexander's brother Nicholas in 1864 but he had died of tuberculosis in 1865. She became known as Maria Feodorovna and had four sons and two daughters including Tsar Nicholas II and the Grand Duke Michael who were both murdered during the Russian Revolution in 1918. She escaped to London in 1919 and eventually returned to Den-

mark where she died in 1928. Her funeral was held at Alexandr Nevsky Church and she was buried in Roskilde Cathedral where she remained until 2005, when her remains were returned to St Petersburg, as she had wished, to be buried next to her husband who had died in 1894.

ALONG THE SOUND

Walk along the Sound, chimneys and windmills visible in the distance, until you reach a copy of Michelangelo's statue of *David*. This heralds the **Royal Cast Collection** ⓫ (Den Kongelige Afstøbningssamling; Vestindisk Pakhus, Toldbodgade 40; tel: 33 74 85 75 (10am–2pm); www.smk.dk; Wed 2pm–8pm, Sun 2pm–5pm; free). Set in an 18th-century warehouse, there are copies of over 2,000 famous statues charting the history of sculpture from Ancient Egypt and antiquity onwards.

A little further on the **Museum of Customs and Taxes** ⓬ (Told Skat Museet; Dahlerups Pakhus, Langelinie Allé 21; tel: 72 37 91 97; Wed, Thur, Sun 11am–4pm; free), in another large, red-brick warehouse, reveals the business of the Sound, Copenhagen's source of wealth over the centuries.

Keep walking until you reach a gate on your left opposite the **pavilions** used by the royal family when boarding their yacht *Dannebrøg*; walk through onto **Esplanaden**. This used to be a busy thoroughfare between the docks and **Nyboder**, Christian IV's naval housing estate built in 1631 *(see p.52)*. On your right stands the statue *Gefionspringvandet*, the 19th-century mock-gothic English **Church of St Albans** as well as the **Frihedsmuseet** (Resistance Museum).

Gefion Statue

Commissioned by Carl Jacobsen in 1909, this **statue ⑬** shows the goddess Gefion driving a plough and four oxen at great speed. She had tricked the Swedish king, who did not know her identity, into letting her have as much land as she could plough in one night, so she transformed her four giant sons and ploughed enough land to create the island of Sjælland (Zealand).

The Resistance Museum

The **Resistance Museum ⑭** (Frihedsmuseet; Churchillparken 7; tel: 33 13 77 14; www.natmus.dk; May–Sep: Tue–Sat 10am–4pm, Sun 10am–5pm; Oct–Apr: Tue–Sat 10am–3pm, Sun 10am–4pm; charge, Wed free) charts the activities of the Resistance during the German Occupation in 1940–45, including sabotage, underground press and the rescue of most of Denmark's Jewish population. Film and recorded interviews and personal memorabilia, including letters and toys, make the period come alive. An execution post is a horrible reminder of the dangers that these people ran.

TOWARDS THE LITTLE MERMAID

Now cross over the bridge by *Gefion* back to the waterside. To your left you will see the grassy ramparts of **Kastellet**, which you can visit later.

There are several statues along here: the first on your left is of Frederik IX (1947–72), Queen Margrethe's father; a little further on is a bronze bust of one Princess Marie, who died young, hence the mourning mother and child at the base of the statue. Other statues along here include *Svømmeren* (The Swimmer), *Efter Badet* (After the Bath), both dating from 1909 and commissioned by the Carlsberg Foundation and *Søfartsmonumentet*, created in 1928 in memory of Danish merchant ships and sailors who perished at sea; the figure on top is based on an ancient statue of Nike from Samothrace. Just before you reach *The Little Mermaid*, you will see a tall pillar, topped by a winged Victory, with cannons and canonballs at its base. This is *Huitfeldtssøjlen* (The Huitfeldt Column), which commemorates Ivar Huitfeldt, a naval captain who died saving many ships in the battle of Køge Bay against the Swedes in 1710.

Continue on and you will come to a group of tourists; behind them you will find *The Little Mermaid* ⑮ (Lille Havfrue), another statue commissioned by the Carlsberg Foundation in 1909. Edvard Eriksen's small, gentle figure

Above from far left: the dome of the Marble Church was inspired by St Peter's in Rome; statues of prophets and apostles surround the dome; the powerful oxen of *Gefionspringvandet*; the unmistakable domes of Alexandr Nevsky Church.

Below: battered armoured car at the Resistance Museum; the Marble Church dome and statue.

Above from left:
the church in Kastellet; the Design Museum explores different themes in both Danish and international design; typical ochre-coloured house in Nyboder.

staring out to sea was modelled on his wife Eline. It dates from 1913. If you are ready for lunch, walk a bit further on along the quayside until you come to **Danish Lunch**, see ⑪③, if you fancy a salad or a sandwich.

Kastellet

Follow Langelinie round, cross the bridge, with the marina on your right, and go down the steps to **Kastellet** ⑯, Copenhagen's star-shaped fort, dating from 1662. It was used fighting the British in 1807 and is now a Unesco World Heritage Site.

It is still used by the army; the **church**, the next-door **prison** and the main **guardhouse** having survived. The Danish Nato headquarters are here and it's the home of Copenhagen's Defence Forces too. Nonetheless, it is a delightfully peaceful enclave, with a charming **windmill** (1847) and some remains of the old ramparts worth seeing.

Towards Nyboder

Walk through Kastellet and you will come back on to Esplanaden near the Resistance Museum. Just opposite stop for a well-earned coffee at **Kafferiet**, see ⑪④, a small coffee shop in a pale-blue, 18th-century town house. If you are looking for something a bit more substantial, turn left up Esplanaden towards the Sound until you reach **Lumskebugten**, see ⑪⑤.

If you want to have a look at **Nyboder** ⑰, carry on down Esplanaden, away from the Sound, until you reach the grid of ochre-coloured houses. The single-storeyed houses date back to 1631; the two-storeyed date from the 18th century and the grey-brick buildings are from the 19th century.

Otherwise turn left down Bredgade, where you will find **Café St Petersborg**, see ⑪⑥, on your left or take the next left onto Store Kongensgade for a Copenhagen institution, **Restaurant**

The Little Mermaid
The Little Mermaid (pictured right) has suffered many indignities in her time, including having her head chopped off – twice. Now, 400m (1312ft) away from the shoreline, she has been reinterpreted as part of a modern sculpture, *Paradise Genetically Altered*, by the controversial artist Bjørn Norgaard.

Ida Davidsen, see ⑪⑦. Just down on your left you'll find two fascinating museums, the **Design Museum** and the **Medical Museum**.

The Design Museum

Set in Frederiksstad's former hospital (1754–1910), the **Design Museum** ⑱ (Kunstindustrimuseet; Bredgade 68; tel: 33 18 56 56; http://kunstindustri museet.dk; Tue–Sun noon–4pm; Wed noon–6pm; charge, under-18s free) is an interesting journey through the history of household design. From Harley Davidsons to cardboard chairs, oriental medieval handicrafts to Rococo furniture, you will be hard pushed not to find something appealing.

Most of the information is in Danish but you can appreciate what you see without too much information. If you are in need of a rest, it has a pretty garden and also an indoor café with good cakes.

The Medical Museum

The **Medical Museum** ⑲ (Medicinsk Museion; Bredgade 62; tel: 35 32 38 00; www.mhm.ku.dk; guided tour only: Wed–Fri 11am (not July–Aug) and 1pm; Sun 1pm; charge) is next door. Although not one for the squeamish, it's a fascinating collection for anyone interested in the peculiarities and horrors of medicine in a bygone age.

Now walk back down to Kongens Nytorv past all the art galleries and auction houses. To end on an indulgent note, pop into **Alida Marstrand**, see ⑪⑧, one of Copenhagen's superior purveyors of hand-made chocolate.

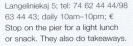

Food and Drink

③ **DANISH LUNCH**
Langeliniekaj 5; tel: 74 62 44 44/98 63 44 43; daily 10am–10pm; €
Stop on the pier for a light lunch or snack. They also do takeaways.

④ **KAFFERIET**
Esplanaden 44; tel:33 93 93 04; Mon–Fri 7.30am–6pm, Sat–Sun 10am–6pm; €
At this tiny coffeehouse, you sit on a stool by the window or at a table outside. The 'double roast' is a speciality.

⑤ **LUMSKEBUGTEN**
Esplanaden 21; tel: 33 15 60 29; Mon–Fri 11.30am–10pm, Sat 5pm–10pm; €€–€€€
Charming, airy restaurant in a former sailors' tavern given to leisurely meals. You may bump into royalty.

⑥ **CAFE ST PETERSBORG**
Bredgade 76; tel: 33 12 50 16; Mon–Fri 11.45am–3pm, 5–8.30pm; Sat 11.30am–4pm; €–€€
Excellent Danish café-restaurant in the beamed basement of a house dating from 1746, part of which used to house the Russian embassy. Go for a *smørrebrød* or a full meal.

⑦ **RESTAURANT IDA DAVIDSEN**
Store Kongensgade 70; tel: 33 91 36 55; Mon–Fri 10am–4pm; €
This *smørrebrød* restaurant is a Copenhagen institution dating from 1888. Over 130 years later, they now serve a choice of 250 sandwiches, which you can eat in or take out.

⑧ **ALIDA MARSTRAND**
Bredgade 14; tel: 45 33 15 13 63; Mon–Fri 10am–5pm
This small chocolatier was first opened in 1930 and the daughter of the original owner still runs it, making everything on the premises.

Above: the charming windmill in Kastellet (1847); Design Museum exhibit.

Nyboder
The inhabitants of Nyboder received free housing and education but in return all boys went to sea for 16–20 years of compulsory service. Naval law applied to the women and children as well as the men.

AROUND ROSENBORG

Rosenborgslot seems remarkable not just for its beauty but also its position bang in the middle of Copenhagen, surrounded by elegant town houses, the botanical gardens and a couple of lovely art galleries.

DISTANCE 2km (1½ miles)
TIME A half/full day
START David Collection
END Hirschsprung Collection
POINTS TO NOTE
If you find yourself short on time, visit Rosenborg Palace and the National Gallery of Art *(see p.60)* and just walk through the King's Gardens and the botanical gardens. The latter make for a welcoming break if you have had your dose of historical artefacts and paintings.

Below: taking a stroll in the King's Gardens.

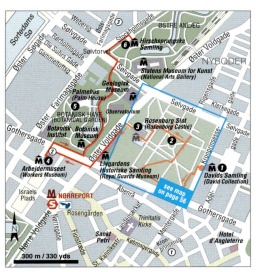

When Christian IV, the architect-king, built Rosenborg, his Dutch Renaissance-style castle, in 1606, it stood not between four urban streets but in the countryside beyond the city's north-eastern ramparts. Christiansborg was a crumbling mess at the time, and Frederiksborg 35km (22 miles) away so it made sense to have a residence closer to the city, yet still in the country. He built it in several stages *(see p.57)* and by 1624, it was much as it is today. It is a highlight for any visitor and still surrounded by its pretty garden, the **King's Gardens** (Kongens Have). Though now reduced in size, this is a welcome green area, especially in summer when the lawns are covered with Copenhagen's citizens in various stages of undress and relaxation. It was first opened to the public in 1771.

The most impressive way to approach the castle is through the gardens from the Kronprinsessegade gate. However, before you go in, take half an hour or so in the **David Collection ❶** (Davids Samling; Kronprinsessegade 30–32; tel: 33 73 49 49; www.davidmus.dk; closed until May 2009 but usually daily 10am–4pm), a lovely collection of European fine arts and Islamic and far-eastern art from the 7th to the 19th centuries.

The collection is housed in an old town house – worth a visit in itself – on a street that, until the fire of 1795, was part of the King's Gardens. After the fire, King Frederik VI donated a strip of land to the city and a long line of neoclassical houses was built. The sale of these financed rebuilding in the Old Town.

If you are in need of a cup of tea afterwards, pop into Copenhagen's oldest teashop, **A.C. Perch Thehandel**, see ⑪①, at No. 5.

KING'S GARDENS

From the entrance to the **King's Gardens ❷** (Kongens Have; winter: daily 7am–5pm, summer: 7am–10pm; free; *see map on p.56*), you will see the best view of the turreted romantic castle, straight down the crocus lawn (finest in spring), lined with marble spheres dating from 1674. The entrance at the end, dating from 1611, is guarded by stone lions and the 'green bridge' over the moat is original and was used by Christian IV to access the gardens.

Wander at will in the gardens or to see it all before visiting the castle, turn left at the entrance and walk around the edge of the park until you come to the second path on your right.

Krumspringet
Turn right and right again to visit the **Krumspringet ❹**, a maze of narrow paths arranged in a symmetrical pattern. This one is modern, but old garden plans show that there was a maze in the gardens back in the 17th century. The name comes from the Danish for 'dodge' because people could avoid unwanted meetings by nipping out of the way down one of its many paths. Walk to the centre and then out again, by the next path on the right, which will bring you to the **crocus lawn ❻**, which is truly spectacular in spring.

Hans Christian Andersen
With the castle on your left, head on down the Allé, towards the **statue of Hans Christian Andersen ❻** at its end. This statue was designed and

King's Gardens
In their early days, the gardens provided the palace with fish from three fish ponds and fruit and vegetables from orchards and vegetable gardens. Even when the castle became state property in 1849, Rosenborg continued to furnish the royal family with fresh produce until 1909.

Below: the crocus lawn in spring.

Above from left:
kids playing football on Israel Plads; the herbaceous border; royal regalia in Rosenborg Castle.

No Kids Allowed
When August Saaybe took the commision for a sculpture of H.C. Andersen, he expected to include children. But Andersen objected, saying that he hated having anyone sitting or standing close to him when he read. He also said that his fairytales were intended as much for adults as for children.

cast during Andersen's lifetime and he had input in to how he was portrayed. It was unveiled in 1880 after Andersen's death. There are some attractive reliefs depicting his stories around the plinth.

Hercules Pavilion and Statue

Turn back and take the first right. Head past a playground and then take the next right to see the **Hercules Pavilion D** and a modern **statue of Hercules and the Lion E** performing the first of his 12 Labours: strangling the Nemean Lion with his bare hands in an attempt to atone for a moment of madness and the murder of his three children.

The pavilion (which is now a café) was built by Christian IV as a place where his family could eat without the servants being present and was originally known as the 'Blue Arbour'. Frederik IV used it to house his sculpture of Hercules, which he bought in 1708–9 on a trip to Italy. Beyond the pavilion is the

herbaceous border **F**, a 20th-century addition to the gardens, which is over 250m (820ft) in length and has over 200 plants that change seasonally.

Now head back to the castle, taking a right and then a left through the **Rose Garden G**, which is laid out in a 16th-century design at the side of the palace. The statue at the end is by the famous sculptor Vilhelm Bissen and depicts Caroline Amalie (1796–1881), wife of Christian VIII, who became queen in 1839. The royal pair were happily married but did not have any children.

ROSENBORG CASTLE

The ticket office is behind the **Rosenborg Castle 3** (Rosenborg Slot; Øster Volgade 4A; tel: 33 15 32 86; www. rosenborgslot.dk; Jan–Apr: Tue–Sun 11am–4pm; May, Sept–Oct: daily 10am–4pm; June–Aug: daily 10am–5pm; Nov–Dec: Tue–Sun 11am–2pm; Mon–Fri guided tours in English; charge) near the entrance on Øster Volgade. If you are not taking a guided tour, buy a guidebook, as there is very little English information inside.

The interior of the castle charts the tastes and needs of different kings from Christian IV in the 17th century to Frederik IV, his great-grandson, in the 18th. It was the monarch's primary residence until 1710, when Frederik IV moved out. Since then, it has been used briefly as a residence on two occasions; in 1794 after the fire at Christiansborg and in 1801, when the British bombarded Copenhagen.

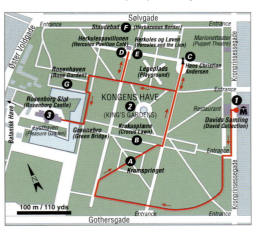

One of the highlights of a trip to Copenahagen, the palace contains the private **royal apartments**, including the bedroom in which Christian IV died in 1648 (having been carried from Frederiksborg expressly for the purpose) and a fully tiled, blue-and-white Delft toilet with an embossed ceiling, and the **State Apartments**, including the **Knights' Hall**, which is packed with solid-silver furniture and countless artefacts alluding to Denmark's success on the world stage.

In the basement, behind massive doors guarded by soldiers, are the Crown Jewels and other exotic royal regalia. The jewels were originally bequeathed for the use of the reigning queen by Queen Sophie Magdalene, 'because', she wrote in her will in 1746, 'in this Royal Family there have been so few jewels, and no Crown Jewels at all'. Items on view here include magnificent jewellery as well as the crowns and insignia of several monarchs.

Before you leave, take a look at the **Pleasure Garden** on the south side of the palace. It is based on the 17th-century original, in which exotic plants were planted to stand alone for dramatic impact.

When you have had your fill, leave by the gate on Øster Voldgade at the back of the castle, and turn left towards Gothersgade. Either cross the road for the entrance to the **Botanical Gardens** or take a short detour down to Gothersgade to visit the **Workers' Museum**.

THE WORKERS' MUSEUM

For the **Workers' Museum** ❹ (Arbejdermuseet; Rømersgade 22; tel: 33 93 25 75; www.arbejdermuseet.dk; daily 10am–4pm; charge) take a right on to Gothersgade and a second left on to Rømersgade, where you will find the museum a short way down on the left.

Housed in the former home of the Danish Workers' Movement, built in 1879 and made redundant in 1979, the museum is dedicated to the history of the worker in Denmark. The four permanent displays focus on daily life, using models and mannequins to tell each story: the 1930s flat belonging to the impoverished, out-of-work Petersen family; the prosperity of the 1950s, seen through the recreation of a coffee shop,

More Renaissance Splendour
Frederiksborg Slot (tel: 48 26 04 39; www.frederiksborg museet.dk; Apr–Oct daily 10am–5pm; Nov–Mar 11am–3pm; charge) is another superb 17th-century castle built by Christian IV, with a lake and Baroque gardens. Take the S train to Hillerød, 40 mins, and bus 701 or 702 from the station.

History of Rosenborg

First built in 1606 by Christian IV as a summer residence, the palace consisted of the core of the south side of the palace that we know today; two storeys high with a spire-crowned turret facing the city and two bays to the east. In 1611, the central gate tower and drawbridge were added. Further work was done in 1613–15, with an additional two-story wing built on the north side of the gate tower; then another floor (containing the Knights' Hall) was added across the whole building in 1616 along with the spire-

crowned towers, and completed in 1624. More work was done ten years later, including an outer double staircase, which was demolished in 1758. The inner staircase, which had connected the first and second floors, was then extended to provide a link with the ground floor.

Botanical Gardens
The first botanical gardens in Copenhagen were founded in 1600. The present ones are the city's fourth and date from 1872.

Below: the elegant Palm House in the Botanical Gardens.

shopping street and typical working family's flat; a two-room flat belonging to the Sørensen family dating from before World War I; and an exhibition on industrial work conditions.

In addition, there is **Café & Ølhalle 1892**, see ⑪②, the workers' original beer hall, which is now a café.

BOTANICAL GARDENS

Return to walk through the **Botanical Gardens** ❺ (Botanisk Have; Øster Farimagsgade 2B; tel: 35 32 22 22; May–Sept: daily 8.30am–6pm, Oct–Mar: Tue–Sun 8.30am–4pm; free), another lovely green space in the middle of the city.

The Botanical Gardens cover 10 hectares (25 acres) and are home to 25,000 plants belonging to 13,000 species. There are lakes and ponds, pretty bridges, plenty of benches with attractive views, a **Palm House** based on the one at Kew Gardens in Surrey, England, and two small museums, the **Botanical Museum** (Botanisk Museum; open for exhibitions) and the **Geology Museum** (Geologisk Museum; Øster Voldgade 5–7; tel: 35 32 23 45; Tue–Sun 1–4pm; charge).

Repair to the café before heading on to your next port of call, the **National Gallery of Art** *(see p.60)*, if you aren't planning a longer visit another day, and the pretty little Hirschsprung Collection, which stands in its grounds.

HIRSCHSPRUNG COLLECTION

Exit the gardens onto Sølvtorvet and turn right for the National Gallery of Art; otherwise, turn left and then left

again up Stockholmsgade for the **Hirschsprung Collection** ❻ (Hirschsprungske Samling; Stockholmsgade 20; tel: 35 42 03 36; www.hirschsprung.dk; Wed–Mon 11am–4pm; charge except Wed). This charming art gallery (housed in a neoclassical villa designed especially for the collection) stands in the sylvan grounds of the Østre Anlæg on the site of the old ramparts of Copenhagen.

The paintings and sculptures, which make up an important collection of Danish art from the period known as the 'Golden Age' (1800–50), was gifted to the nation in 1902 by tobacco tycoon Heinrich Hirschsprung (1836–1908). It is an intimate museum with the art displayed as it might be in a private residence, surrounded by period furniture and artefacts from the artists' homes and studios. Artists featured include those from the Skagen group, the Symbolists and C.W. Eckersberg, who is credited with laying the foundations for the art of the Golden Age in Denmark.

Something to eat is most likely to now be on your mind. You could check out the good but rather pricey café in the National Gallery of Art or, better still, walk back down to Sølvtorvet and up Øster Farimagsgade until you reach **Aamanns Deli**, see ⑪③, one of Copenhagen's newest and most modern *smørrebrød* restaurants.

The Golden Age

The Danish Golden Age spanned the first half of the 19th century and was a time of new ideas and great creativity in the arts. The leading proponents all lived in Copenhagen, then a small city of 10,000 inhabitants, and would have known each other and exchanged ideas. Ironically, as art and culture flourished, Denmark was suffering economically and politically. Important cultural figures at this time were the artist Christofer Eckersberg who introduced a new naturalism and intimacy to painting; C.F. Hansen, the inspired classical architect, who was responsible for rebuilding many of Copenhagen's buildings after the 1795 fire; the great fairytale writer Hans Christian Andersen (*see also p. 44*); the philosopher Søren Kirkegaard; the ballet choreographer August Bournonville; and the sculptor Bertel Thorvaldsen.

Food and Drink

② CAFE & ØLHALLE 1892
Rømersgade 22; tel: 33 33 00 47; 4.30am–4pm; €
A good selection of Danish food and beer, including 'Stjerne (Star) Pilsner' that still bears the original 1947 label.

③ AAMANNS DELI
10 Øster Farimagsgade; tel: 35 55 33 44; Mon–Fri 10.30am–8pm, Sat 11am–4pm; €
Fabulous organic café with classy decor offering innovative *smørrebrød*.

6

THE NATIONAL GALLERY OF ART

The Statens Museum for Kunst, or Kunstmuseum as it is also known, is Denmark's national art gallery. Housed in a building that reflects two centuries of design, its world-class collection spans 700 years of national and international art.

Bringing Kids

Children are very welcome at the museum; ring ahead or ask at the reception desk about activities on offer. If you have a buggy with you, you must leave it outside, but you can borrow covers and locks to secure it with from reception. You can then borrow one of the museum's buggies from the entrance hall. Lockers are also available for bags larger than A4 size.

DISTANCE n/a – the whole tour is spent within the museum

TIME A half/full day

START Level 1: Sculpture Street

END Level 2: Rooms 212–16

POINTS TO NOTE

This vist can be as short or as long as you like to make it. At a fairly brisk pace, you can cover most of it in about two hours, but you will enjoy it more if you give it a bit more time.

You cannot fail to be impressed the minute you walk into Denmark's **National Gallery of Art** (Kunstmuseum; Sølvgade 48–50; tel: 33 74 84 94; www.smk.dk; Tue, Thur–Sun 10am–5pm, Wed 10am–8pm; free). Its high, airy foyer, winding staircase and view through to the collections beyond are the result of an impressive redesign and the removal of a large central staircase in the 1960s.

LEVEL 1

To get your bearings and to explore the mix of old and new architecture, walk through the entrance hall, down the steps to **Sculpture Street ❶**, which runs across the back of the old 19th-century building in a new glass-roofed extension. To the left and right, with no protection from wayward feet and fingers is a marvellous collection of modern sculpture, the most arresting is perhaps controversial sculptor Jørgen Haugen Sørensen's threatening and viscious collection of dogs, *That's why they call them dogs* (2002–4).

Directly ahead is a set of wide steps, actually the seats of an **amphitheatre ❷**. At the back of its stage is a glass wall, through which you can see the water and greenery of Øster Anlaeg, the park at the back of the museum. Through a door to the left (as you look towards the garden) is a small **children's museum-cum-activity area ❸**, aimed at kids aged 0–6. There is a series of **workshops ❹**, where creativity can be explored, just above it; enter via the stairs on Sculpture Street.

LEVEL 2

The second level is home to the collections. To follow this tour, take the lift on the left of the amphitheatre in

Sculpture Street to level 2, coming out by room 269c. Now turn left down to Room 260.

Foreign Art 1300–1800

Rooms 260–270c ❺ are dedicated to international art from the early Renaissance onwards. Do not expect this to be a simple chronological display; a new rehanging of the Old Masters has been themed, sometimes mixing old with new for contrast and the correlation of ideas. **Room 260** takes Mythology as its theme; check out the delicacy of the butterfly placement in Cornelisz van Haarlem's *Fall of the Titans* (1599–90) and Michael

Kvium's grotesquely blunt, naked *Choir* (1991). Next door, in **Room 261**, is some of the work of Adrien de Vries (1556–1626), a Dutch Mannerist sculptor. **Room 262** showcases Deception and Illusion, a theme especially popular in the 17th century, with examples of painstaking and detailed *trompe l'œil*. Oddly enough, in terms of colour and subject matter, many of these are reminiscent of Cubist works created two centuries later. Don't leave without checking out the easel and canvas in the far left-hand corner of the room; you will be surprised.

On the other side of the corridor, look into **Rooms 270a**, **b** and **c**, where you

Above from far left: the original building dates back to 1896; the interior of the museum has been redeveloped to allow for more of the collection to be displayed with better lighting and space; sculpture in the museum gardens.

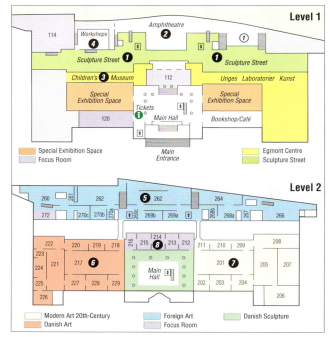

Collection History
The original collection, once the private collection of the king, first went on show to the public in 1822 at Christiansborg Palace. Fortunately, it escaped the palace fire in 1884 and the National Gallery of Art, designed by Vilhelm Dahlerup, was opened in 1886. The new extension dates from 1998.

Information on the Works
There is no audio tour available, but all rooms offer introductory texts that describe what is in the room. There are also a number of information cards that describe key works on show.

Danish Art
If you like Danish 19th-century art, visit the Hirschprung Collection *(see p.59)* in the museum's grounds. It has an excellent collection, including some lovely works by the Skagen School.

will find an interesting collection of statuettes, the stunning *Portrait of Martin Luther*, a personal friend of the artist Lucas Cranach, dating from 1532 at the height of the Reformation in Europe; and an eerie and unnerving installation *Please Keep Quiet!* (2003). It's so realistic that you will wonder whether you are doing the right thing by going through the closed door.

Walk back up the corridor, past the lift and into, on your left, **Room 263**, dedicated to Art Genres. Here, paintings have been hung according to their subject matter, which makes for some interesting comparisons. There is English labelling at the bottom of each wall. On the left wall as you come in, look out for two works by Anthony van Dyke (1509–1641), a study, *Head of a Young Man* and a *Portrait of a Lady* (1638–40) and, on the other side of the partition wall opposite, an *Adoration of the Kings* by Hans Memling (*c.*1433–94).

Along the corridor on the left, **Room 264** holds 700 years of portraiture; the earliest piece a donor portrait in an altar panel by Petrus Christus dating from 1450, the latest, Peter Carlsen's jovial, slightly surreal *Golden Tongues* of 2005. There are also two portraits by El Greco (1541–1614); one of a bug-eyed man with a rubbery face by Frans Hals (1581/5–1666); portraits of *Francesco de' Medici* and *Joanna of Austria* by Rubens (1577–1640); and a couple of busts by Gian Lorenzo Bernini (1598–1680). By way of contrast, don't miss Kurt Trampedach's sculpture, *Sleeping Man in a Chair* (1976–7) next to some seemingly traditional portrait busts by

controversial artist Christian Lemmerz, which, on closer inspection, show faces disintegrating. Another quirky but effective addition to the gallery are the mirror and accessories that encourage visitors to experiment with their own representation and image.

Room 265, the small area behind Rooms 264 and 267, takes the 18th-century European Grand Tour as its theme and has some lovely paintings by Italians Tiepolo and Guardi and Frenchmen Nattier and Fragonard.

At the end of the corridor, **Room 266** is an example of the museum's – at times – unorthodox hanging policy, putting abstract artist Richard Mortensen (see also room 208) in counterpoint with Rubens' masterpiece, *The Judgement of Solomon*, dated 1617.

Heading back down the other side of the corridor, **Rooms 268a** and **268b** display examples of Renaissance and Gothic art, including the lovely *Meeting of St Anne and St Joachim at the Golden Gate* by Filipino Lippi (1457–1504) and a portrait by Titian (1489–1576) of his mentor, Venetian painter Giovanni Bellini. **Room 269a** displays works by Rembrandt and his followers and **269b**, flower paintings, contrasting 17th-century Dutch paintings with five large works by modern artist Erik A. Frandsen; **Room 269c** has miniatures.

Danish Art 1750–1900

Go through the glass doors by the lift, crossing a bridge over Sculpture Street, back to the original 19th-century museum building. Turn right into **Rooms 217–29 ❻**, a section dedicated

to Danish art that includes the period 1800–50, an era known as the Golden Age *(see p.59)* in which the arts flourished, new ideas and styles came to the fore, and, in the arts, a turning to nature and the everyday condition of the world and its inhabitants, was paramount. **Room 217**, straight ahead, will give you an overview of the period.

Highlights of this section of the museum include the rather ominous *Evening Talk* (1863) by the anxiety-laden Edvard Munch and the trademark-grey *Seated Female Nude* (1889) by Vilhelm Hammershøi in Room 217; the delightful *Boys Bathing on the Beach at Skagen* and *Summer Evening* (1899) by P.S. Krøyer, an important painter from the Skagen school; Svend Wiig Hansen's work, *The Earth Weeps* (1981), in Room 221; the naturalistic works of Michael Ancher, P.S. Krøyer and others, depicting the harsh realities of working-class life in Room 227; and Room 228 honours Vilhelm Hammershøi. Room 229 deals with the theme of Mental Breakthrough with a focus on death, especially poignant in Munch's *Death Struggle* (1915) and tuberculosis-sufferer Ejnar Nielsen's raw and mesmerising *And in his Eyes I saw Death* (1897), in which a hollow-eyed figure looking like a young Omar Sharif waits by a coffin, staring hopelessly at the future that awaits him.

20th-Century Modern Art

Come out of Room 229 into the gallery that runs around the open foyer below. Go down the right side towards

Rooms 202–211 ❼. **Room 202** takes an interesting look at the relationship between abstraction and representation. What does a painting that doesn't represent anything represent? Have a look at Georg Brandes' *Crema* (2004). At first glance, it suggests a dead body, shoe soles facing the viewer, in a snowy wood. Its label explains that it is upside down and shows a road leading to the Italian town of Crema; when it is explained you can see it but you would be hard put to work it out.

For an overview of the period, step into **Room 201**. Highlights in this section include several works by Matisse (1869–1954) in **Room 203**, including the especially famous *Portrait of Madame Matisse* (1905), also known as *The Green Line*, which gave rise to the

Above from far left: *Untitled* by Peter Land (2003); contemporary latex art display.

Below: *Portrait of Madame Matisse*, *The Green Line* (1905) by Henri Matisse.

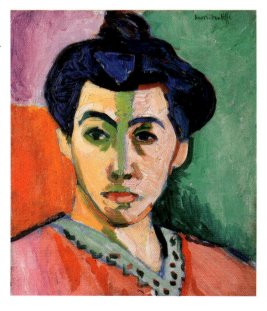

name of the French splinter art group, The Fauves (or 'wild animals'), whose work was characterised by a strong use of intuitive colour. Emil Nolde's disturbing Expressionist painting of *The Last Supper* (1909) is in the same room. For an *embarras de richesses* of great early 20th-century art by legends such as Picasso, Modigliani, Léger, Braque, Gris, Dufy, Derain and Soutine, visit **Room 204**. **Room 205** covers a similar period in Denmark and, having seen the art in room 204 and other earlier rooms, it's very interesting to see how ideas and styles spread and were used outside Paris.

Political art is featured in **Room 206** and includes works on film, notably the iconic *Female Christ at the Stock Exchange* (1969) and *Horse Sacrifice,* both by Bjørn Norgaard. Both caused a huge furore in their day and, even now, are daring and challenging works.

Don't miss **Room 208** dedicated to the CoBrA group, a collective of artists from Copenhagen, Brussels and Amsterdam, and considered to be one of the most important groups to emerge after World War II. Their art tended towards the surreal, with an abstract distortion of images often borrowed from primitive and folk art, and their technique shows an expressive emphasis on colour and intense brushwork. Jorn's *Orange Object* (1944) shows a monster with teeth and his almost fairytale-like *Wheel of Life* (1953) is a universal and timeless theme that he took up after recovering from tuberculosis in 1951.

Another of Denmark's greats, Per Kirkeby (b.1938) is showcased in **Rooms 212–16 ❽**. Don't miss the video in **Room 214**, in which you can see the artist creating *Winter Picture* (1996), which is on the wall behind you. In commenting on his thought processes as well as the progress of the painting, he rather comfortingly tells us that if he makes a mistake, 'it doesn't matter much; I can always paint over it.' Unless you are on a mission, now have a rest and revive yourself with a visit to the café, see 🍴①, on Level 1.

Food and Drink 🍴

① CAFE REPUBLIC
Level 1; tel: 33 74 86 65; Tue–Sun 10am–5pm, Wed 10am–8pm (kitchen closes one hour before museum; €–€€
Lovely fresh food, all cooked on the spot and served in stylish surroundings. Lunch plates start at 95dkk.

NØRREBRO AND ALONG THE RESERVOIRS

The main things to do in Nørrebro are walking in the cemetery on a nice day and meandering around the shopping streets around Sankt Hans Torv. Weather-permitting, the reservoirs are a pleasant spot for a walk or jog.

Nørrebro (North Bridge) lies beyond the reservoirs. As in Vesterbro *(see p.26–31)*, construction here began in the 19th century. It is a popular, alternative place to hang out or shop.

Start on the city side of **Dronnings Louise Bro ❶** (Bridge), which dates from 1887; note the statues of Neptune. On your left is **Peblinge Sø** (lake), while on your right is **Sortedams Sø**.

Walk down Nørrebrogade and turn left on Blågardsgade passing through **Blågards Plads ❷**. This was once an avenue leading up to Blågård Castle, which burnt down in 1833. On your left, note the statues along the edges of the sunken square, where there may be a few beer drinkers hanging out. The carvings date from 1913–16 when they were carved on site by sculptor Kai Nielsen using the locals as his inspiration. Cross the square and turn right up Korsgade as far as Kappelvej. Turn right at Helligkors Kirke, following the street around until you reach the entrance to the cemetery on your left.

ASSISTENS KIRKEGARD

This **churchyard ❸** (May–Aug: daily 8am–8pm, Sept–Oct and Mar–Apr: 8am–6pm, Nov–Feb: daily 8am–4pm;

DISTANCE 4.5km (2¾ miles)
TIME A half day
START Drønnings Louise Bro
END Tycho Brahe Planetarium
POINTS TO NOTE
It's a long walk from the centre, so take a bus from Rådhuspladsen to Dronnings Louise Brø.

free) is very popular with the locals, especially in summer, when you will see plenty of joggers, sunbathers and mothers with buggies. It was laid out in 1760 to relieve pressure on the city graveyards, which were full to overflowing after several outbreaks of plague had killed over one third of the population (23,000 people) in just 50 years. For a map and list of famous graves, including H.C. Andersen, Niels Bohr and Dan Turréll, turn right at the entrance. For Hans Christian Andersen *(see p.44)*, turn left.

Come out of the same gate and turn left and then right onto Nørrebrogade. Cross the road and walk down to **Elmegade ❹**, a popular shopping street. Browse in the likes of Goggle, ILove and Foxy Shoes for clothing and accessories. If you are in the mood for

Above: the Tycho Brahe Planetarium cuts a striking figure behind the reservoirs.

Start at Either End
You can start this walk in Nørrebro and walk back to the inner city taking in the Tycho Brahe Planetarium, or you can start at the Planetarium and spend the afternoon/evening in Nørrebro. Either way, stop for a drink to take in the local atmosphere.

Above from left:
laundry and lattes at the Laundromat Café; the solar system in the Planetarium; leafy Fredericksberg; outdoor ice-skating.

a coffee or a bite to eat, drop into the **Laundromat Café**, see ⑪①, at No. 15 or keep on until you reach **Sankt Hans Torv ❺**, the central place to hang out in summer. Here, **Pussy Galore's Flying Circus**, see ⑪②, is popular. Cross the square, walk down Sankt Hans Gade, and turn right on to

Ravnsborggade ❻, which is full of bric-a-brac and antique shops. At the end, turn left onto Nørrebrogade. Just before Dronning Louise Bro, turn right down **Peblinge Dossering ❼**, stopping to enjoy the view from one of many reservoir-side benches. Turn left for a glass of wine at the waterside café **The Front Page**, see ⑪③.

Continue on down the side of the last reservoir (look back for a lovely view of all five reservoirs); at the bottom is the **Tycho Brahe Planetarium ❽** (Gammel Kongevej 10; tel: 33 12 12 24; Mon–Fri 9.30am–9pm, Sat–Sun 10.30am-9pm; charge), which has some interesting displays and a fantastic IMAX cinema.

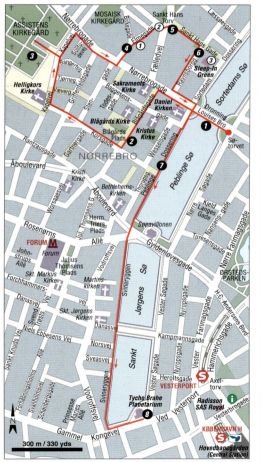

Food and Drink

① LAUNDROMAT CAFE
Elmegade 15; tel: 35 35 16 72; €
One of Copenhagen's new 'hybrid' cafés; in this case, you can do you your washing and buy second-hand books while having a coffee.

② PUSSY GALORE'S FLYING CIRCUS
Sankt Hans Torv 30; tel: 35 24 53 00; www.pussy-galore.dk; Mon–Fri 8am–2am, Sat–Sun 9am–2am; €–€€
Average food but very popular for its retro decor and tables outdoors.

③ THE FRONT PAGE
Sortedam Dossering 21; tel: 35 37 38 27/29; Mon–Wed, Sat 11am–1am; Thur–Fri 11am–2am, Sun 10am–1am; €–€€
Attractive decor and reasonable food. The real appeal is the pontoon on the lake, where you can sit and watch the swans.

FREDERIKSBERG

Leafy Frederiksberg is Copenhagen's upmarket – formerly royal – suburb, and home to Frederiksberg Slot, Søndermarken and the underground Glass Museum, the zoo and attractive, tree-lined, residential boulevards. Although so close to the centre, it is a municipality independent of Copenhagen.

Until the 18th century, Frederiksberg was a small country village. It rose to prominence as the concept of a country retreat began to appeal to middle-class and wealthy town dwellers. There had been a small royal farm at the end of Frederiksberg Allé since 1663 but in 1703 Frederik IV started construction on the castle that now stands on the hill to the south.

This walk starts at **Frederiksberg Runddel ❶**, in front of the park gates. Every winter (Nov–Mar), there is an outdoor skating rink here. This is not far from the junction of Vesterbrogade and **Frederiksberg Allé**, formerly the rather grand private road that led to the castle. When you walk along this major boulevard you will pass several theatres, a war memorial and **Frederiksberg Chokolade**, an excellent chocolate shop, see ⑪①. As you approach the *runddel* (square), you will pass a cemetery on your left belonging to **Frederiksberg Church**. To visit the church, turn left onto Pile Allé.

FREDERIKSBERG CHURCH

Frederiksberg Church ❷ (Frederiksberg Kirke; Frederiksberg Allé 65; daily 8am–5pm), with its pyramidal roof, was built in the Baroque style by

DISTANCE 2km (1¼ miles)
TIME A full day
START Frederiksberg Runddel
END Memorial Mound
POINTS TO NOTE

This walk works well in both directions – in summer the zoo is open late, so it makes sense to go there last; in winter you may want to go there first. You can also tack this walk, or part of it, onto the Vesterbro walk (*see p.26–31*). Turn right at the top of Ny Carlsberg Vej, cross the road and up some steps into Søndermarken. Follow the path to Frederiksberg Castle and the zoo.

architect Felix Dusart in 1732–34 and is notable for its octagonal shape, the first of its kind in Denmark. Inside,

Short Detour
If you haven't visited Copenhagen's gourmet food street on the Vesterbro walk, take a few moments before you start to have a look and turn right up Værnedamvej.

Food and Drink ⑪

① FREDERIKSBERG CHOKOLADE
Frederiksberg Allé 64; tel: 33 22 36 35; Mon–Thur 10am–5pm, Fri 10.30am–6pm, Sat 10am–2pm; €€
Exquisite handmade cakes and chocolates. Highlights include 'golden balls', brushed with 18-carat gold, and 70 per cent chocolate body paint. Also runs courses, if you want to learn their secrets.

Above from left:
Frederiksberg Gardens
are home to many
species of birds;
Frederiksberg Castle;
a Chinese bridge.

The Dummy Tree
Generations of
Danish children
have consigned
their last dummy
to the branches of
the Dummy Tree
in Frederiksberg
Gardens.

there are four attractive, green-painted wooden galleries, which were added in 1864. Many important Danes are buried in the graveyard, including figures from the Danish 'Golden Age' (1800–50, *see p.59*), such as the poet Adam Oehlenschläger *(see p.31)* and his children.

ALLEGADE

Before entering the park opposite, turn right and walk up **Allegade ❸**, a pretty street lined with restaurants and cafés set back from the road. This is one of Frederiksberg's oldest streets, dating from the 1650s when the first farmers settled here. Since the end of the 18th century, it has also been the place to have fun and in 1784, there were 34 pubs ranged along here. **Allegade 10** on your left and **Lorry** and **Grock** opposite date from this period.

On your left, as you walk up, there is also the **Museum of Danish Revue**

Theatre ❹ (Revymuseet; Allegade 5; tel: 38 10 20 45; Thur–Sun 11am–4pm; charge), housed in a yellow-stone villa behind a white picket fence.

STORM P MUSEUM

Return to Frederiksberg Runddel, where you will find the main entrance to the park. On the left is a delightful small museum, the **Storm P Museum ❺** (Storm P Museet; Frederiksberg Runddel; tel: 38 86 05 23; May–Sept: Tue–Sun 10am–4pm, Oct–Mar: Wed, Fri, Sun 10am–4pm; charge), which is dedicated to Storm P.

This witty Danish cartoonist's work seems to combine the social realism of the late 19th and early 20th centuries with the ludicrous inventions of Heath Robinson and some of the cartoon qualities of Mr Magoo. Marvellous if you understand Danish, but still worth popping in for the visual style and humour even if you do not.

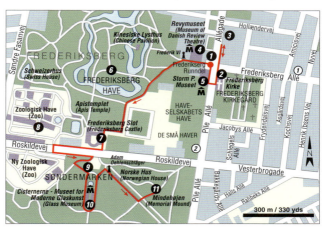

FREDERIKSBERG GARDENS

If lunch or supper is looming, visit one of the small, very traditional Danish restaurants called 'De Små Haver' (The Small Gardens), next to the Frederiksberg Gardens (Frederiksberg Have), before you go any further. **M.G. Petersens Gamle Familiehave**, see ⑪②, is the only one to be open all year-round.

Enter the **park** ❻ through the main gate (daily: Dec–Jan: 7am–5pm, Feb and Oct–Nov: 7am–6pm, Mar: 7am–7pm, Apr and Sept: 7am–9pm, May–Aug: 7am–10pm; free). In the 19th century, there used to be a guard here charged with keeping out anyone he considered undesirable (including seamen and people with dogs).

Just inside the gates there is a **statue of King Frederik VI** (1808–39) by H.W. Bissen. Frederik VI, cousin to Britain's king, George VI, governed as Regent from 1784 and was responsible for abolishing serfdom in 1788. He was also Regent during the British attacks on Copenhagen in 1801 and 1807. The inscription on the plinth translates as, 'Here he felt happy in the midst of loyal people'.

There is a park map at the entrance. To the right, you will find yourself walking around the canal system within the park. Turn left and you walk along the side of the park, towards Frederiksberg Castle and the zoo (this is the quickest route).

The park was originally a formal Baroque garden but in 1798–1892 was remodelled in the fashionable English 'Romantic' style. There are several follies dating from 1800–50, notably the **Chinese pavilion** (Jun–Aug, Sun 2–4pm; free; cross by the ferry boat), the **Møstings House**, a listed, pretty neoclassical house, the **Swiss House**, a little cottage built for the royal family to take tea, and the colonnaded **Apis Temple**. Close to the Chinese pavilion, there is a colony of grey herons – the males arrive in March and the females in May – they can often be seen wandering the lawns and paths.

Frederiksberg Castle ❼ (Frederiksberg Slot; closed to the public), standing at the south end of the gardens, is now a military academy. Walk up to its terrace and admire the view along the broad axis that is part of the original Baroque design. In the 19th century, you could see as far as the Sound from here.

Leave via the exit on the other side of the castle and turn right, to walk down until you reach the zoo. The park opposite is **Søndermarken**, and the far end of Vesterbro *(see p.26)* lies on the other side.

Above: the Chinese pavilion where, in the 19th century, Frederik VI took afternoon tea with his family; Frederiksberg Gardens are an oasis of tranquillity.

Food and Drink 🍴

② M.G. PETERSENS GAMLE FAMILIEHAVE
Pile Allé 16; tel: 36 16 11 33; www.petersensfamiliehave.dk; daily 11am–11pm; €–€€
Traditional *smørrebrød* and lunch platters at reasonable prices are served in comfortable surroundings that date back to 1858. The music events held here are also great fun.

Above from left:
lions and zebra at the zoo; the NY Carlsberg Glyptotek; mother and child in the Glyptotek's Winter Garden.

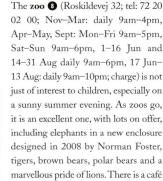

Above: the zoo also hosts elephants (in their brand new enclosure), baboons, prairie dogs and brown bears *(right)*.

Famous Danes
The Glass Museum contains art works created by some of Denmark's most famous modern artists including, Per Kirkeby, Carl Henning Pedersen, Bjørn Nørgaard and Robert Jacobsen.

THE ZOO

The **zoo** ❽ (Roskildevej 32; tel: 72 20 02 00; Nov–Mar: daily 9am–4pm, Apr–May, Sept: Mon–Fri 9am–5pm, Sat–Sun 9am–6pm, 1–16 Jun and 14–31 Aug daily 9am–6pm, 17 Jun–13 Aug: daily 9am–10pm; charge) is not just of interest to children, especially on a sunny summer evening. As zoos go, it is an excellent one, with lots on offer, including elephants in a new enclosure designed in 2008 by Norman Foster, tigers, brown bears, polar bears and a marvellous pride of lions. There is a café and a snack kiosk close to the entrance.

SØNDERMARKEN

Opposite the zoo is another garden **Søndermarken** ❾ (daily 24 hours; free). The **Glass Museum** is in sight of the road, the entrance marked by a glass pyramid, and the **Memorial Mound** is down a path to your left.

Glass Museum

The **Glass Museum** ❿ (Cisternerne – Museet for Moderne Glaskunst; weekends and public hols 11am–5pm; also Mar–Oct: Thur–Fri 2pm–6pm, Nov and Feb Thur–Fri 2pm–5pm; charge) is worth a visit for its location alone. Housed in an underground water tank built after the cholera epidemic of 1853, its arches stretch out in all directions like a crypt, water occasionally drips gently from the ceiling, lifesize limestone statues loom out of the darkness at you and richly decorated modern stained-glass works glow in the gloom. It's an atmospheric, almost medieval, experience that you are unlikely to find anywhere else.

Memorial Mound

Walk back towards the castle and turn right. You will pass a **statue of the poet Adam Oehlenschläger**, who ran around the park as a child because his father was the Palace Steward, and the **Norwegian House**, a romantic folly dating from 1787, before reaching the **mound** ⓫ (open 4 July only) on your left. It is surrounded by tall trees and commemorates Denmark's emigrants. The words above the entrance translate, 'They who set out, never to return'. Inside, at the end of a stone passage, there is a cavern, a cupola letting in light above the life-size figure of a woman representing Mother Denmark, who is embracing her children.

The easiest way to get back to the centre of town is on the No. 6 bus from outside the zoo.

MUSEUMS AND PLEASURE GARDENS

For a lovely day and evening of culture and fun, this is an excellent circular walk, taking in up to three art galleries and museums during the day and Tivoli, Copenhagen's historic pleasure gardens, in the evening.

NY CARLSBERG GLYPTOTEK

This tour begins on the steps of the **Ny Carlsberg Glyptotek ❶** (Dantes Plads 7; tel: 33 41 81 41; www.glyptoteket.dk; Tue–Sun 10am–4pm; charge except Wed and Sun), a wonderful art gallery housing the collections of Carl Jacobsen (1842–1914), son of the founder of Carlsberg beer. His taste was predominantly for the ancient and classical and with his wife Ottilia, he built up one of the world's best collections of Egyptian, Greek, Roman and Etruscan art. Much of the world-class modern collection showcasing the Impressionists, Post-Impressionists and Danish 19th-century art was built up after his death.

Level 1

As you pass through the impressive porticoed façade, you can see through

> **DISTANCE** 1.5km (1 mile)
> **TIME** A full day
> **START** Ny Carlsberg Glyptotek
> **END** Tivoli
> **POINTS TO NOTE**
> It's easy to spend a day in the Glyptotek so keep an eye on the time if you want to visit the other museums as well.

to the grand, airy 19th-century **Winter Garden**, strewn with plants and statues and home to the museum's excellent café, see ⑪①. Directly ahead are the steps to level 2; at the far end on the left is the entrance to the modern extension.

Level 2

Level 2 is home to the **Greek and Roman Collections**, the **Egyptian collection** and **19th-century French and Danish sculpture**. Among many other treasures, including a whole room dedicated to **Rodin**, this is the place to come for an intimate picture of the faces of the past, including such notaries as Alexander the Great, his father Philip of Macedonia, the Roman emperors Caligula (still with traces of ancient paint on the face), Augustus

Food and Drink 🍴

① CAFE GLYPTOTEK
Tel: 33 41 81 28; Tue–Sun 10am–4pm; €–€€
Lovely salads and light lunch dishes but especially popular for its cakes.

A 'Glyptotek'
For Carl Jacobsen, sculpture was the most important art form and the word 'glyptotek' means 'a collection of statues'.

Above from left:
designer chairs in the
Dansk Design Center;
the Greek and Roman
collection at the Glyp-
totek; ethnic masks at
the National Museum.

Gift to the Nation
Carl Jacobsen gave
his collection to the
nation in 1888 on
the understanding
that the state built a
suitable building for it.
When the first part
was opened in 1897,
it lay in open country
with a view to the
east across the
swampy environs
of the harbour.
Jacobsen thought
it rather remote and
inappropriately close
to plebeian Tivoli.

and Hadrian. Don't miss the atmospheric Egyptian collection, which you enter down steps as if in to a tomb. Among the startling collection of artefacts are some wonderful sarchophagi plus painted models of tombs and scenes of Egyptian daily life.

The Modern Wing

The modern wing, designed by the architect Henning Larsen, houses a beautiful collection of **Etrurian and Mediterranean art** and an impressive **French collection**, which includes works by artists such as Gauguin, Degas, Monet, Manet, Bonnard, Van Gogh, Cézanne, Renoir, Pissarro and Berthe Morisot. Look out for Degas' statue of a 14-year-old dancer, Manet's *Absinthe Drinker* (1859), Van Gogh's *Landscape from St Rémy* (1889) and Gauguin's *Skaters in Frederiksberg Gardens* (1884), dating from the time

(1883–4) that he and his Danish wife and family lived in Copenhagen.

DANSK DESIGN CENTER

Cross the road and visit the **Dansk Design Center** ❷ (H.C. Andersens Boulevard 27–9; tel: 33 69 33 69; www.ddc.dk; Mon–Tue and Thur–Fri 10am–5pm, Wed 10am–9pm, Sat–Sun 11am–4pm; charge except Wed) for one of their exhibitions on cutting-edge design. The striking building is the work of architect Lars Henning. There's also another good café here, the **Café Dansk**, see ⑪②.

NATIONAL MUSEUM

The next port of call is the **National Museum** ❸ (National Museet; Ny Vestergade 1; tel: 33 13 44 11; www.natmus.dk; Tue–Sun 10am–5pm;

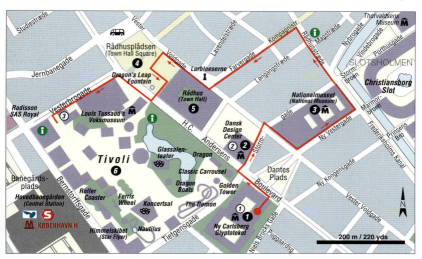

charge except Wed), Denmark's national cultural collection. Walk down Stormgade, take a right on Vester Voldgade and first left down Ny Vestergade. The museum is a little way down on the left.

The collection ranges from the prehistoric period to the modern day in Denmark and also includes a wonderful ethnographic collection. The ground floor is home to prehistory and the children's museum. The first to third floors can be confusing but the rooms all run around the atrium with ethnography, coins and medals, the Middle Ages and the state rooms on the first floor; the history of Denmark (1660–2000) and more ethnographic collections (including those of the Inuit) on the second floor; and Near Eastern and Greek and Roman antiquities on the third floor.

Ground Floor

The museum's amazing **prehistoric exhibition** includes unique archaeological treasures such as the **Gundestrop Cauldron**, thought to show scenes of human sacrifice and one of the world's few depictions of the Iron-age god Cernunnos; the **Trundholm Chariot of the Sun**, dating from *c*.1200 BC, when the Danes worshipped the sun, imagining it riding through the sky in a chariot pulled by a celestial horse; and the fascinating **Egtved grave** belonging to a blonde young woman wearing a string skirt, bodice, dagger and hairnet. A companion grave belongs to a young man with a full head of hair and rings in his ears.

First Floor

As you come up the stairs from the atrium, facing towards the street, the **Danish Middle Ages and Renaissance** is located on your left and an **ethnographic collection** on the right.

The two collections are, in many ways, similar; both vast, both charting the social and religious practices of a time and place, from minute articles to entire rooms and houses. (Both collections also continue directly above on the second floor.) Don't miss the **Royal Apartments** (Rooms 127–134), including the marvellous **Great Hall**, which date from the 1740s when the building was still a royal palace, home to the Crown Prince Frederik V.

The ethnographic collection on this floor includes artefacts from **Africa**, **India**, **Indonesia**, **New Guinea**, **New Zealand**, **Japan**, **China**, **Central Asia** and **Siberia** as well as a **music room** featuring world music and a fascinating slide presentation.

RÅDHUSPLÅDSEN

From the National Museum, turn left. At the bottom of Ny Vestergade you'll

Tiniest and Oldest
The museum's tiniest exhibit is a shoe carved from a cherry pip. It is part of the original royal collection. You can also see Denmark's oldest coin, minted at the behest of Sweyn Forkbeard, Harald Bluetooth's son, about 1,000 years ago.

Tivoli Ride Tickets
To go on any of the rides you need to either buy a multi-ride pass (3–11s 160dkk; over-12s 200dkk), which lasts all day, or separate tickets (10dkk); rides need two–six tickets each. If you have a Copenhagen card *(see p.107)* and just wish to wander, this will let you in for free.

Below: the *Lurbloeserne* stands tall on Rådhuspládsen.

find the Frederiksholms Kanal and the island of Slotsholmen *(see p.76)*. For Rådhuspládsen turn left again and third left onto Farvergade Kompagnistraede, home to the astronomer Tycho Brahe in 1597, until you come to **Rådhuspládsen ❹**.

The square, which dates from the start of the 20th century, is now a large space surrounded by hotels and restaurants, with the bus terminal in its middle. It plays an active part in city life and is the site for Christmas and New Year festivities, concerts and, in January 2008 was the starting post for the Monte-Carlo Historic Rally. It is dominated by the town hall or Rådhus, dating from 1905 after the town hall

on Nytorv *(see p.33)* became too small for the city's needs. In front of it is the **Dragon's Leap Fountain**, designed in 1923 by Joachim Skovgård (1856–1933); next to it the *Lurbloeserne*, a 12-m (40-ft) column topped with two Viking horn-blowers dating from 1914. Sculptor Siegfried Wagner (1874–1952) took a few historical liberties as the horns are Bronze Age and precede the Vikings by over 2,000 years. You can see original examples in the National Museum *(see p.72–3)*.

Town Hall

The **Town Hall ❺** (Rådhus; Rådhuspládsen 1; tel: 33 66 25 82; Mon–Fri 8am–5pm; free; tours in English Mon–Fri 3pm, Sat 10am and 11am; charge includes climbing the tower) was built in mock-Gothic style by architect Martin Nyrop in 1905. A statue of Bishop Absalon and fantastical sea creatures adorn the façade. Inside, the entrance hall is a flurry of pseudo-Renaissance splendour with golden mosaics and a minstrels' gallery. Visitors can climb the splendid **clock tower** (Mon–Fri 10am–4pm, Sat 10am–1pm; charge) for an excellent view of the city and also see **Jens Olsens Verdensur**, which, according to *Guinness World Records*, is the world's most accurate clock and is said to have over 14,000 parts. If it is sunny or you just need a place to sit down, there is a pretty **garden** (daily 10am–4pm) with benches behind the Town Hall. Walk down either side of the building and walk through the first open gateway that you reach.

Food and Drink 🍴

③ THE PAUL
Tivoli; tel: 33 75 07 75; www.thepaul.dk; Apr–Sept: Mon–Sat; €€€–€€€€
A real treat. Delicious food in a stylish but welcoming, homey atmosphere. The six-course set lunch and dinner menus here change regularly.

TIVOLI

To visit **Tivoli** ❻ (Vesterbrogade 3; tel: 33 15 10 01; ticket booking 33 15 10 12; www.tivoli.dk; mid–Apr–mid–Sept: daily 11am–late, Oct: 12–21 daily 11am–11pm; mid–Nov–Dec: Sun–Thur 11am–10pm, Fri–Sat 11am–11pm; charge), cross H.C. Andersens Boulevard by the writer's statue to the entrance opposite.

Founded in 1843 outside the city walls, Tivoli is as popular now as it has ever been with over five million visitors every year. Ignore the cynics, this is a great day or night out whether you go on the rides or not. There are plenty of rides for adults and kids alike – the former rather more stomach-churning and scream-inducing than the latter. For the hardy, there are four roller coasters, one of which travels at speeds of up to 80kmh (50mph), the **Dragon**, which

moves in several directions at once and **Himmelskibet**, the tallest carrousel in the world, which twirls its riders up to 80m (260ft). The **dragon boats** on the lake, the **pantomime theatre**, the **Tivoli boys guard**, trees and lakes all lit with Chinese lanterns have a romantic appeal for non-adrenalin junkies.

There is also lots of music and drama here: the **concert hall** is one of the best in Copenhagen offering ballet and opera (buy tickets in advance); the **open-air stage** sees loud, free rock and pop concerts every Friday night; and the pantomime theatre is free, as are the many musical groups playing on bandstands throughout the park.

If you get peckish, there are 32 restaurants to choose from ranging from budget to top-end, including the Michelin-starred **The Paul**, see ⑪③, or bring a sandwich. Alternatively, sit on a bench and people watch.

Above from far left: the bright lights of Tivoli; the Town Hall far and close-up; up, up and away in Tivoli.

Tivoli – i lov iT
There are plenty of rides for the kids, including a Viking-ship merry-go-round, flying aeroplanes, miniature classic cars, an old-fashioned trolley bus ride and a traditional carrousel. The newest ride is the Nautilus, a roundabout based on *20,000 Leagues under the Sea*.

Left: Tivoli is a collage of architectural styles that includes Chinese pagodas, Moorish palaces and everything in between.

10 SLOTSHOLMEN

Slotsholmen is the oldest site in Copenhagen for it was here, in 1167, that Bishop Absalon built a castle to protect the little fishing village of Havn from the unwanted advances of German pirates. A castle has stood here ever since and, 900 years later, the island is still the centre of national government.

DISTANCE 2km (1¼ miles)
TIME A full day
START Palace forecourt
END Black Diamond
POINTS TO NOTE

This route is not the most leisurely, packing in lot of sights, especially if you stop for lunch. It's a great day for busy sightseeing, though.

This is the fifth castle to stand on Slotsholmen (Castle Island). The first was a fortress surrounded by a limestone wall; it lasted 200 years before it was destroyed in 1367 by the Hanseatic League, a German alliance of trading guilds that monopolised trade in the Baltic and Northern Europe.

The second castle was built in 1375; in 1417 it gained in importance when the Danish king, Erik of Pomerania,

Holmens Kirke
Holmens Kirke (Mon-Fri 9am–2pm; Sat 9am–noon; free) is another of Christian IV's projects. It was originally a naval forge but was converted into a church for the navy in 1619. Queen Margrethe was married here in 1967.

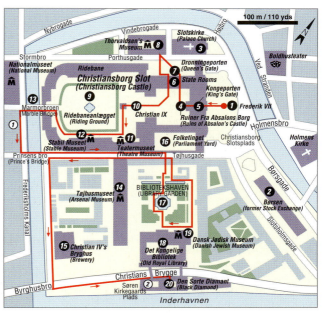

made Kjøbmandehavn (now Merchants' Havn, reflecting its growing commercial success) his state capital. It was enlarged over the years but by the 18th century was falling down – something commented upon by visiting dignitaries – and Christian VI, mindful of his position razed it to the ground.

The third castle, a beautiful Baroque palace, was erected between 1731 and 1745 but it fell victim to fire in 1794 and only the magnificent stables and intimate red-and-gold theatre escaped the flames *(see p.79)*. Homeless, the royal family repaired to the mansions of the aristocratic elite at Amalienborg from which they never returned *(see p.47)*.

Between 1803 and 1828 a fourth castle, designed by the classical architect C.F. Hansen, was built. Used for ceremonial occasions and entertaining, in 1848 it, too, went up in smoke, with just the Palace Church and the Riding Ground left standing.

The fifth and current castle was built between 1907 and 1928 by Thorvald Jørgensen who, mindful of the fate of its predecessors, built its walls of reinforced concrete with granite facings. It is home to the State Rooms, the Folketinget (Parliament), Prime Minister's Office and Supreme Court.

SLOTSHOLMEN IN A DAY

Before you enter the castle through the main gate, facing Holmens Kirke *(see margin, p.76)*, take a look in the forecourt at the **equestrian statue ❶** by Vilhelm Bissen, which represents Frederik VII (1808–63). Note, too, the building on your left with the twisted spire. This is the **Stock Exchange ❷**, (Børsen; closed to the public but you can take a virtual tour at http://english.borsbygningen.dk), built in 1618–24 by Christian IV, who wanted to make Copenhagen a great trading centre *(see p.82)*. The building was constructed with many doors on a narrow dam with water on both sides, so that goods could be unloaded directly into the building from ships. It originally housed a simple hall, which had storage space on the ground floor and booths and offices on the upper floor. In 1625, Christian enhanced the building by adding 18 gables and a 54-m (177-ft) spire, made up of four entwined dragons' tails, said to protect the building. The three golden crowns on top represent Denmark, Norway and Sweden.

It did not become a stock exchange until the mid-19th century. The traders are now long gone, and the building is used as offices.

Above from far left: aerial view of Slotsholmen; the castle close-up.

Danish Parliament
The sessions of the Danish Parliament are open to the public. The Folketing can be found in the southern part of the main palace and is open Tue–Fri at 1pm. Enter through Parliament Yard.

Below: Neptune stands guard next to the Stock Exchange.

Above: Palace Church pews; Theatre Museum mannequin; the statue of Victoria, the goddess of victory, on top of the Thorvaldsen's Museum.

Royal Prisoner
Princess Leonora Christina was a favourite daughter of Christian IV. She spent almost 22 years in the Blue Tower after her husband Count Corfitz Ulfeldt plotted against the new king, Frederik III. Ulfeldt was accused of treason in 1663 but died before he could be executed.

Right: Thorvaldsen's Museum.

If you are visiting on a Sunday, between noon and 4pm, now would be a convenient time to make a short detour to visit the **Palace Church** ❸ (Christiansborg Slotskirke, Christiansborg Slotplads; tel: 33 92 64 51; www.ses.dk/christiansborgpalace; free), the neoclassical building with the portico, on your right.

The present church, a lovely, light, airy affair, was built by C.F. Hansen between 1813 and 1826 after its Rococo predecessor burnt down in 1794. Almost 200 years later, in June 1992, during Whitsun Carnival, it was beset by fire again, its cupola and dome crashing to the floor. It has now been restored to international acclaim.

The Ruins of Absalon's Castle

Alternatively, visit the **ruins of Absalon's Castle** ❹ (tel: 33 92 64 92; May–Sept: daily 10am–4pm, Oct–Apr: Tue–Sun 10am–4pm; charge), which will give you an idea of the size as well as the history of this site. The entrance is on your right as you enter through the **Kings Gate** ❺, which was part of the fourth palace. As well as the remains of the walls, houses, a bakery and Absalon's chapel, you will be privy to Absalon's 'secret', an ancient toilet, through which detritus washed into the Sound. Look out, too, for a wooden pipe, which was part of a system of hollowed-out tree trunks that brought fresh water to the castle from Lake Emdrup 6km (4 miles) away. There are also some remains of the second castle, including the foundations of the terrible 'Blue Tower', in

which prisoners, noble and plebeian alike, could be holed up for years.

The State Rooms

The **State Rooms** ❻ can only be visited by tour (in English May–Sept: 11am, 1pm, 3pm, Oct–Apr Tue–Sun 3pm) and are reached via the **Queen's Gate** ❼, which dates back to the time of the fourth palace. The tour includes the **Throne Room**, the **Dining Room**, the **Royal Chambers**, the **Great Hall** with tapestries by Bjørn Nørgaard, and the **Queen's Reference Library** lined with roughly 3km (2 miles) of shelving. It's well worth a visit and the guides are so enthusiastic that if you weren't before, you are bound to be a royalist by the time you finish the tour.

Thorvaldsen's Museum

If you are interested in classical 19th-century sculpture, from here, walk through Prince Jørgens Gård bearing

left to reach the **Thorvaldsen's Museum ❽** (Bertel Thorvaldsens Plads 2; tel: 33 32 15 32; www.thorvaldsensmuseum.dk; Tue–Sun 10am–5pm; charge, Wed free) on the far edge of the island, on Gammel Strand *(see p.37)*. This brightly painted museum, its exterior depicting a life-size scene of the great sculptor's triumphant homecoming from Italy in 1838 after an absence of 40 years, houses virtually the entire collection of Bertel Thorvaldsen (1770–1844). His plans, casts, originals and replicas, plus his antiques – including examples of Egyptian, Greek, Etruscan and Roman works – and his collection of paintings, are all here. He is buried in the courtyard at the centre of the museum, which opened in 1848.

The Riding Ground

Back in the Inner Courtyard, look up at the tower that dominates the palace roofline; at 106m (348ft), it is one metre taller than the Town Hall and thus the highest in Copenhagen.

Now walk through to the **riding ground ❾**, which survived the fire of 1848. The equestrian statue, complementing the one in the palace forecourt, depicts **Christian IX ❿** and is the work of sculptor, Anne Marie Carl Nielsen (1863–1945), wife of the Danish composer Carl Nielsen.

Theatre and Stable Museums

The Theatre and Stable Museums are under the arcade on the left-hand side of the riding ground. Both were part of the third palace and the sole survivors of the fire in 1794.

The **Theatre Museum ⓫** (Christiansborg Ridebane 18; tel: 33 11 51 76; www.teatermuseet.dk; Tue and Thur 11am–3pm, Wed 11am–5pm, Sat–Sun 1–4pm; charge, under-18s free) is not to be missed. One of the oldest court theatres in the world, it was designed by the French architect Nicolas-Henri Jardin and has been restored to how it would have looked in its sumptuous heyday between 1767 and 1881, when it was a stage for opera and drama. On a dramatic note, it is here that Christian VII's powerful adviser Struensee *(see box below)* was arrested for treason. Enhanced with mannequins and music, visitors can

Above from far left: the impressive Throne Room; a collection of costume dresses from the Theatre Museum; Bjørn Nørgaard's tapestries hang in the Great Hall.

The King's Doctor

Johan Struensee (1737–72) was a German doctor who was influenced by the revolutionary ideas of the Enlightenment. Convinced he had a greater calling than that of a mere physician, he sought preferment at court and, in 1767, became travelling doctor to the mentally unstable king, Christian VII. He gained the affection and trust of the young king and by September 1770, had been given the senior post of Privy Counsellor. By this time, he was also the lover of Queen Caroline Matilde (sister of George III, King of England), which caused great scandal. Until his downfall in January 1772, he ruled Denmark in the king's name, zealously, introducing over 1,000 reforms. But he was resented and his reforms met with disfavour. In January 1772, he was arrested, accused of usurping the royal authority in contravention of the royal law. He was imprisoned in Kastellet and executed on 28 April 1772.

Above: Stable Museum exhibit.

Palace Bridges

To reach Christiansborg Palace, you can cross one of four bridges. The Rococo Marble Bridge (Marmorbroen; *pictured below*) is the oldest (1744) and was part of Christian IV's Baroque palace. Originally the pavements were of Norwegian marble, hence the name.

wander backstage, through the boxes, and stand on the stage, surrounded by props and other memorabilia.

The **Stable Museum** ⓬ (Christiansborg Ridebane 12; tel: 33 40 26 77; May–Sept: Fri–Sun 2–4pm, Oct–Apr: Sat–Sun 2–4pm; free) next door houses the collection of state coaches and carriages in palatial, marble-columned surroundings that kept the king's horses in equine splendour. An astonishing 270 horses were housed here in 1789; now there are about 20 of them, and they can occasionally be seen in their stalls.

The Arsenal Museum

Turn left and walk towards the **Marble Bridge** ⓭. Cross over and have a bite at **Kanal Kafeen**, see ⓰①, or wait until you get to the Black Diamond.

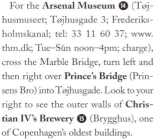

For the **Arsenal Museum** ⓮ (Tøjhusmuseet; Tøjhusgade 3; Frederiksholmskanal; tel: 33 11 60 37; www.thm.dk; Tue–Sun noon–4pm; charge), cross the Marble Bridge, turn left and then right over **Prince's Bridge** (Prinsens Bro) into Tøjhusgade. Look to your right to see the outer walls of **Christian IV's Brewery** ⓯ (Brygghus), one of Copenhagen's oldest buildings.

The museum, about two-thirds of the way down on your right, is housed in a splendid brick building dating from 1598, which used to be Christian IV's cannon hall. The 163-m (535-ft) hall, reputedly the longest in Europe, is worth a visit for the building alone, not to mention the museum's staggering, internationally renowned collection of weaponry ranging from daggers to cannons, Hawk missiles to exquisitely inlaid duelling pistols.

Old Royal Library and Jewish Museum

Come out of the Arsenal and turn right down to **Parliament Yard** ⓰. Go through a door on your right where you will find an attractive **garden** ⓱, complete with pond and statuary (Søren Kirkegaard is on the right). At the far end is the **Old Royal Library** ⓲, dating from 1906.

The **Jewish Museum** ⓳ (Holmens Kanal 2; tel: 33 11 22 18; www.jewmus.dk; Sept–May: Tue–Fri 1–4pm, Sat–Sun 10am–5pm, Jun–Aug: Tue–Sun 10am–5pm; charge; children free), opened in 2006 and charts the life of the Jewish community in Copenhagen from the 17th century, when immigrants were

rather aristocratic, to just before World War II, when lower-class sections of society began to arrive to escape the hardships of Eastern Europe. The exhibition does not cover the Holocaust or World War II; this is covered at the Museum of Danish Resistance 1940–5 (Frihedsmuseet; *see p.51*).

The museum is also remarkable for its stunning interior, by the architect Daniel Libeskind. The design comprises interlocking sections, many of which tilt to one side, which are intended as a metaphor for the amicable history of the Jewish community and the Danes.

Black Diamond

The **Black Diamond** ❷ (Den Sorte Diamant; Christians Brygge 1; tel: 33 47 47 47; Mon–Fri 10am–5pm, Sat 10am–2pm; free) is the modern extension of the Royal Library and can be found on the opposite side of Christians Brygge, behind the old library building. Walk round via Tøjhusgade.

It opened in 1999 and takes its name from its shiny black exterior and slanting silhouette. It is best seen from a boat *(see p.46)*. See the press for details of exhibitions from the library's archives, which include original manuscripts by H.C. Andersen, Søren Kirkegaard and Karen Blixen. It is also home to the National Museum of Photography (with regular temporary exhibitions) and the Queen's Concert Hall. If you haven't had lunch yet, head to the minimalist, fat-free and very good **Søren K**, see ⑪②, on the ground floor.

see p.51; *see p.46*

Above from far left: canon line-up at the Arsenal Museum; a dainty carriage at the Stable Museum; the old library building and garden.

Christian IV's Brygghus

Christian IV's brewery was originally built as part of Copenhagen's fortifications before it was turned into a brewery to supply beer to the navy.

$50 Million Book Theft

Some 4.5 million books are a lot to keep track of as Frede Møller-Kristensen, an employee of the Royal Library's Oriental department, realised. Between 1968 and 1978 he removed 3,200 items, including manuscripts by Martin Luther and first editions by Immanuel Kant, Thomas More and John Milton; nobody noticed until 1975. Møller-Kristensen sold over two million dollars' worth of books and remained undetected until his death in 2003. But his family were careless in selling the remainder and their cover was blown when books belonging to the library appeared at auction at Christie's in London. When the family house was raided in November 2003, 1,500 books were found. The family received sentences of between 18 months and three years each.

Food and Drink 🍴

① KANAL KAFEEN
Frederiksholms Kanal 18; tel: 33 11 57 70; 9am–9om; € (cash only)
Hearty local food, including *smørrebrød* in warm and cosy wood-beamed surroundings.

② SØREN K
Søren Kirkegaard Plads 1; tel: 33 47 49 49; Mon–Sat noon–midnight (kitchen closes 10.30pm); €€€€
Come for the delicious food (French-Danish fusion) and the wonderful view through the large windows overlooking the harbour.

CHRISTIANSHAVN AND HOLMEN

Christianshavn is one of the city's most colourful areas and the closest you will get to seeing how Copenhagen looked before the fire in 1728. It was created as a harbourside merchant town to help promote trade.

Sea View

Harbour tours run from Nyhavn and outside Holmens Kirke *(see p. 76)* and take you to Opera House and along Christianshavns Kanal, with Overgaden Oven Vandet (Upper Street Over the Water) and Overgaden Neden Vandet (Upper Street Below the Water) on either side, before crossing over to Slotsholmen *(see p. 76).*

DISTANCE 3km (2 miles)
TIME A full day
START/END Knippel's Bridge
POINTS TO NOTE
If you find yourself short of time, an appealing way to see some of Christianshavn is to take a harbour tour *(see margin left).*

Christian IV wanted to make Copenhagen the cultural, religious and business centre for the whole of the Nordic region and, as such, needed to enhance the naval and trading capabilities of the city.

Between 1618 and 1623, he had fortifications built in the swampy area between Copenhagen and the island of Amager. Five bastions were completed by 1623. By 1639 he decided that he wanted to build a town and gave the order for Christianshavn (Christian's Harbour) to be built, allowing for dockyards and warehouses alongside the merchant housing. He was so determined for this new city to be populated that he offered many of Copenhagen's wealthy merchants independence, free land, 12 years unrestrained by taxes and several other incentives to up sticks from their comfortable homes and business premises on the mainland and settle here instead.

His experiment worked and by the time he died in 1648, Copenhagen had become the naval and economic centre of the region.

CHRISTIAN'S CHURCH

Start at the green-towered **Knippel's Bridge ❶** (Knippelsbro), the site of the first bridge between the mainland and Amager Island. Built in 1937, it is named after Hans Knipp, the toll-keeper of the first bridge erected in 1618. Note the six black, shiny buildings on your right, designed by the architect Henning Larsen, in stark contrast with the old-world atmosphere of the rest of the area. Walk up as far as Strandgade and take a left and walk down to Christian's Church.

Christian's Church ❷ (Christians Kirke; Strandgade 1; tel: 32 96 83 01; Mar–Oct: 8am–6pm, Nov–Feb: 8am–5pm; free) is one of two splendid churches on Christianshavn. It was built in 1755–9 by Nicolai Eigtved, Frederik V's master architect, who designed many of Copenhagen's 18th-century churches. This elegant Rococo

church is notable for its unusual, theatrical layout in which seating galleries run around the walls at a second level, with the royal pew in the centre opposite the altar, technically in the position of the 'stage'. The church was first named for Frederik V (Frederiks Kirke) but in 1901 the name was changed to reflect the importance of Christian IV. The tower was added in 1769 by Eigtved's son-in-law G.D. Anthon.

STRANDGADE AND THE DOCKS

Walk back up to Torvegade and cross over into **Strandgade** ❸. This elegant 17th-century street was the one of the earliest, and **Nos 30** and **32** were the first houses to be built here. They were built by the mayor of Copenhagen, Mikkel Vibe, and originally had curved attic gables similar to those adorning Rosenborg Castle; these have since been replaced by an additional storey. The painter Vilhelm Hammershøi *(see p.97)* lived at No. 30 between 1899 and 1909, producing many of his trademark grey-tone interiors here.

When this street was first built, it was right on the shoreline, as its name, Beach Street, suggests, with jetties and with gardens leading down to the water. The closer to the water (and Copenhagen) you were, the smarter the address.

Go through a wooden door on the left, opposite Sankt Annæ Gade, into

Above from far left: capturing serene Christianshavn.

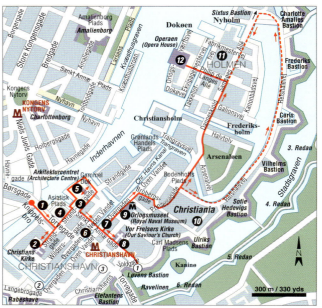

Below: Christian's Church adornments.

Above: Our Saviour's Church altarpiece; tranquil Christianshavn.

The Order of the Elephant
This is an ancient order and the highest in Denmark. It was instituted in its current form in 1693 by Christian V. Royalty and heads of state may belong; commoners occasionally receive the honour. The industrialist A.P. Møller is the only living commoner to be a member. Nicolas Ceaucescu, late former Romanian dictator, is the only person to have had the honour revoked.

Asiatisk Plads ❹. This is named for the Asiatisk Kompagnie, which traded with India and China from here in the 18th century. It was also responsible for commissioning and paying for the excessively expensive statue in the Amalienborg Plads *(see p.49)*. On the north side, the marble façade of the elongated Rococo warehouse was designed by Nicolai Eigtved in 1750 and dates from Christianshavn's heyday. It is now a conference centre.

Walk past the lovely old boats and bear right, past the end of the next building into **Gammel Dok** (Old Dock). On the far side is the **Architecture Centre** ❺ (Arkitekturcentret; Strandgade 27B; tel: 32 57 19 30; www.dac.dk; Thur–Tue 10am–5pm, Wed 10am–9pm; free), Denmark's foremost exhibition centre for new architecture. Housed in a lovely old converted warehouse with exposed beams, it has constantly changing exhibitions. It also has a good bookshop and its café has an excellent waterside view. Further up on **Grønlands Handels Plads** opposite Nyhavn, the warehouses belonged to the Royal Greenland Trading Company (Kongelig Grøn-

landske Handel) and were used to store whale oil, skins and dried fish. There was then, and still is now, a Greenlandic population in Christianshavn.

Back on Strandgade, walk down Sankt Annæ Gade; note **No. 32** on the corner, thought to be the oldest house in Christianshavn, dating from *c*.1622. When you reach the canal, **Overgaden Neden Vandet** ❻ (Upper Street Below the Water) is on your left and **Overgaden Oven Vandet** ❼ (Upper Street Above the Water) on your right. These are two lovely cobbled streets overlooking the houseboats on the **Christianshavn Canal**. Cross the bridge and head towards **Our Saviour's Church**, with the twisting, golden spire.

OUR SAVIOUR'S CHURCH

Our Saviour's Church ❽ (Vor Frelsers Kirke; Sankt Annæ Garde 29; tel: 32 54 68 63; www.vorfrelserskirke.dk; spire Apr–Aug: daily 11am–4.30pm; Sept–Oct: daily 11am–3.30pm; free) is the oldest church in Christianshavn, built by Christian V for the inhabitants of the new harbour district between 1682 and 1694. Dedicated to Our Saviour, it is a wonderful example of Dutch Baroque style and is particularly well known for its spiralling tower, which twists to a height of 90m (295ft).

The view from the top of the external stairway is exhilarating but the climb is not for the unfit or acrophobic. Above you is a golden ball and a statue of Christ that is 3m (10ft) tall. This magnificent spire replaced the original square one in 1749–52.

Food and Drink 🍴
① **BASTIONEN AND LØVEN**
Lille Mølle Christianshavn, Voldgade 50; tel: 32 95 09 40; www.bastionen-loven.dk; noon–midnight; €–€€€
This charming restaurant is in an old mill on the ramparts of Christianshavn. It serves excellent Danish food and is especially popular for its weekend brunches (10am–2pm).

Inside is a light-filled, white-walled church with tall windows in the shape of a Greek cross. The cherub-covered font has a sad history: it was given by Frederik IV's childless, morganatic wife in 1702; she died in childbirth in 1704, and her baby died nine months later. The altarpiece, inspired by the altar in the Roman church of S.S. Domenico e Sisto, shows God (represented by the sun) and the events of Maundy Thursday, when Christ prayed that he should be spared the crucifixion. Christian V's insignia can be seen on the entrance, the ceiling and the three-storey organ, which rests on two elephants, the emblem of Denmark's most prestigious order *(see margin left)*, founded in 1450. The pulpit dates from 1773 and is decorated with figures of the apostles.

Turn left out of the church and walk to the end of the road; bear left up onto the fortifications, and on your right is one of Christianshavn's best restaurants, **Bastionen and Løven**, see ⑪①.

ROYAL NAVAL MUSEUM

Retrace your steps and walk down Overgaden Oven Vandet, passing the **Royal Naval Museum** ❾ (Orlogsmuseet; Overgaden Oven Vandet 58–64; tel: 33 11 60 37; www.orlogsmuseet.dk; Tue–Sun noon–4pm; charge except Wed) on your right. Although there's little information in English here, there are some beautiful 17th-century model ships to admire, as well as uniforms, nautical instruments and weapons, which are well worth seeing. The long, Rococo-style building was formerly used as a school, a prison, a hospital and then a rehabilitation centre for wounded naval personnel.

CHRISTIANIA

If you wish to visit **Christiania** ❿, take Brobergsgade, the second right after the Royal Naval Museum, and then keep walking until you end up

Above from far left: the view from Our Saviour's Church; walking through Christiania; the spiralling tower of Our Saviour's Church; Christiania mural.

Left: young skater showing off his skills.

Night at the Opera
To go to the opera house directly from the centre, take harbour buses Nos. 901 or 902 from Nyhavn, or the metro to Christianshavns Torv and the No. 66 bus; a water bus also runs after each performance, but queues can be long, and the No. 66 might be a better bet if you find yourself at the back of the queue.

on Prinsessegade. Opposite is the colourful mural-covered entrance to Copenhagen's 'Free State', a 19th-century, ex-army barracks that was taken over by freethinkers in 1971.

Christiania is home to just over 1,000 people, out a population in Christianshavn of 9,000. To get the most out of it, take a tour (www.christiania.org); just wandering around can be a little underwhelming.

HOLMEN

From here retrace your steps and take a right up Prinsessegade. The quickest thing to do here is to wait for a No. 66 bus, which will take you up to near the **Opera House** on Holmen. Alternatively, take a right on to Refshalevej and walk up along some of the

bastions though this will take you a good half hour at least.

Holmen ⓫ is made up of five man-made islands (now connected by bridges), which were created from 1690 for the royal navy. It is built on muddy landfill that was dredged up by convicts who walked in huge treadmills in the waterway between Copenhagen and Amager. Eventually, the authorities supplied a horse-drawn dredger. Parts of the islands rest on ships that have been sunk and filled with boulders.

Nyholm, the first island, was built to replace the naval dock at Gammelholm, which had become too small and the water too shallow for the navy's fleet of ever-larger and faster ships. The **Sixtus Bastion** at its far end is still the place from which cannon are fired in salute, and there are several unique historical buildings still standing.

Once Holmen was a working naval base, its workers came across the water every day from Nyboder (see p.53). They were considered so important that during the plague in 1711–12, which killed a third of the population, they lived in huts on Nyholm to keep them away from infection.

The navy remained on Holmen for three centuries until it finally, and regretfully, moved out in 1989. Since then, the area has seen an increase in public spaces and housing and is now also home to four art schools and a brand new, impressive opera house.

Opera House
Opposite the Amalienborg is Copenhagen's exciting new **Opera House**

(Operaen; Ekvipagemestervej 10; tel: 33 69 69 69; www.operaen.dk; charge for guided tours only). Opinions regarding its strikingly contemporary design (by Henning Larsen) vary, especially with regard to its controversial position on the 'Golden Axis' with the Amalienborg and the Marble Church on the other side of the Sound. But whatever the critics say, the building is impressive, standing 14 storeys high (five underground), with a flat grey roof that blends in with the sky.

Inside, a large glass-fronted foyer looks out over the water, lit by several huge, one-tonne lamps by Danish-Icelandic artist Olafur Eliasson, who constructed them from thousands of pieces of glass that change colour depending on the temperature. In the centre, the main auditorium is encased in Canadian walnut and looks like a huge wooden pumpkin. Inside, it is a masterpiece of acoustic design, with an elaborate gold-leaf ceiling made of over 100,000 pieces of 23.75-carat gold.

The building took four years to build and was a gift to the nation by Denmark's richest citizen, industrialist A.P. Møller. The behind-the-scenes tour is very interesting; the areas you see depend on rehearsal schedules, but there are over 1,100 rooms in the building, so you won't be stuck for something to see. If you are lucky you will get to stand on the stage itself.

From here, hop on a harbour bus and go back to Knippel's Bridge. While away the rest of the time you have in the local shops and cafés, notably **Café Rabshave**, see ⑪②, and **L'Altro**, see ⑪③.

Above from far left: the maritime way of life at Christianshavn is still there for all to see; the striking new Opera House opened in 2005.

Holmen 5
The five islands that make up Holmen are Nyholm, Dokøen, Frederiksholm, Arsenaløen and Christiansholm.

Below left and right: the stylish interior of the Opera House is a showcase of modern Danish design.

Food and Drink 🍴

② CAFE RABSHAVE
Ved Kanalen; Wed–Sun 11am–8pm, (lunch 11am–4pm, supper Wed only; €
This atmospheric pub is slightly off the beaten track and dates from the 17th century when it catered to the soldiers manning the local bastions. Nice atmosphere, pretty garden, good organic food.

③ L'ALTRO
Torvegade 62; tel: 32 54 54 06; www.laltro.dk; Mon–Sat 5.30pm–midnight (kitchen closes at 10pm); €€
Owned by the same brothers who own nearby Michelin-starred Era Ora, this offers excellent, traditional, home-made Italian food.

ROSKILDE

Seaside Roskilde is a relaxing day out just 25 minutes away by train. It is considerably older than Copenhagen and for centuries was much more important. This walk takes you to the town's highlights, the cathedral and Viking Museum, via many ancient sights and then back through the park.

Tourist Information

If you want to visit the tourist information office, note that it is on Bredgade, just off Allehelgensgade. To reach it from the station, turn left and walk as far as Allehelgensgade. Turn right, then left (into Bredgade). Retrace your steps to Allehelgensgade and turn left up to the main square and the cathedral. When you come back from the Viking Museum, take a left down Domkirke Stræde at the east end of the cathedral and follow the early part of the walk that you missed, back to the station.

Roskilde is thought to have been founded in the 900s by the splendidly named Harold Bluetooth (Harold I) of Denmark, a Viking who converted to Christianity *c*.AD 960. It is well placed at the bottom of a fjord, and tucked away but with access to the North Sea. Harold established his court here and also built a church on the site of the current cathedral.

By 1020, Roskilde was a bishopric, and in 1158, Bishop Absalon, who later founded Copenhagen, became bishop of Roskilde. He established several more churches and monasteries, until there were 14 parish churches and five convents and monasteries in addition to a brick church on the site of the present cathedral. In the Middle Ages,

Roskilde was one of the largest, most important cities in Northern Europe, with between 5,000 and 10,000 inhabitants and thousands of visiting pilgrims each year.

TO THE CATHEDRAL

From the Italian-inspired station, which dates from 1847, turn right up Jerbanegade. The wall on your left encloses **Gråbrødre Kirkegård ❶**, an attractive church surrounded by a graveyard now used as a park, which stands on the site of a 13th-century complex belonging to the Franciscans. Take a look at the beautiful view through the gates or turn left down Store Gråbrødretorvstræde if you want to enter the park.

Walk across cobbled Hestetorvet ❷ named for the horse market that was held here in the 12th century, just inside the ramparts by the eastern gate, where you cannot miss the **Roskilde Jars**. These are the work of artist Peter Brandes and stand 5m (16ft) high and weigh 24 tonnes. They were gifted to the city in 1998 on its 1,000th anniversary by a local firm, and, as they are both storage jars and urns, represent Life and Death.

Pass between the café and the pharmacy to the shopping street, **Aldgade** ❸, an ancient street that has been paved for over 700 years; you can see some medieval paving just beyond the Hotel Prindsen. Keep an eye out, too, for No. 9, an old merchant's house opposite the imposing red-brick Dom Apotek. There is a good family restaurant **Bryggergården**, see ⑪②, at No. 15; go through its archway to see the timbered backs of the old houses. Also, have a look through the gates of No. 31 to see the back of the Old Priory, which you will see shortly at closer quarters. Take a right up Sankt Peders Stræde until you reach **Roskilde Priory** on your right.

Roskilde Priory

Roskilde Priory ❹ (Roskildekloster; Sankt Peders Stræde 8; tel: 46 35 02 19; www.roskildekloster.dk; by tour only, ring for details; charge), dates from 1565 and was built as a manor house on the land of the Dominican (Blackfriars) Priory, which is thought to have stood just northwest of this site since the 13th century. The priory was destroyed during the Reformation in 1536, and its bricks sold off for building in the area; some may have been used for this building too. The manor house is built in Dutch Renaissance style and has an interesting history as a home for unmarried mothers of rank; despite their shame, they lived in great style, as a tour of the Great Hall, abbey church and reception rooms will show.

Roskilde Museum

Out of the Priory, cross the road and walk down Sankt Ols Stræde; you can see the spires of the cathedral ahead of you. Turn right at the end and the **Roskilde Museum** ❺ (Sankt Ols Gade 18; tel: 46 31 65 00; www.roskilde museum.dk; daily 11am–4pm; charge)

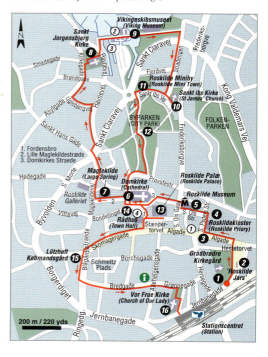

is on your right. The museum offers over 6,000 artefacts relating to the history of Roskilde and nearby Lejre, from prehistoric times until the 1970s, including the founding of the annual Roskilde rock festival *(see margin left)*.

THE CATHEDRAL

From here, cross over Sankt Ols Gade into Domkirkes Stræde. Turn left and pass in front of the cathedral for the main entrance; visit now or on your way back from the Viking Museum.

The **cathedral** ❻ (Domkirke; Apr–Sept: Mon–Fri 9am–4.45pm, Sat 9am–noon, Sun 12.30pm–4.45pm, Oct–Mar: Tue–Sat 10am–3.45pm, Sun 12.30pm–3.45pm; closed during services; charge; tours Sept–Mar: Tue–Fri noon, 1pm, Sat noon; Sun 1pm, 2pm, Apr–mid-Jun: Mon–Fri 11am, 1pm, 2pm, Sat 10am, Sun 1pm, 2pm, mid-Jun–Aug: Mon–Fri every 30 mins from 11.05am to 2.35pm, Sat every 30 mins from 9.05am–11.35pm, Sun every 30 mins from 1.05–3.35pm) is a Unesco World Heritage Site and one of the earliest brick-built buildings in Northern Europe. Pick up an information sheet on your way in so you have a plan of the building.

Work on the church began in the 1170s, under Bishop Absalon, but the building was completed by his successor Peder Sunesøn, who was aware of the new Gothic style that was then emerging in France. (Indeed, this is one of the earliest Gothic buildings outside France.) The cathedral is famous for being the resting place of the 39

Danish monarchs who have ruled since the Middle Ages; their chapels and tombs are a fascinating display of changes in style. There are also **pillar tombs** in the sanctuary behind the choir, of royals originally buried in the two, possibly three, earlier churches that have stood on this site. These include Harold Bluetooth and Estrid, Canute's sister, who built the first stone church here in the 11th century after her brother murdered her husband Ulf in the previous timber church.

Inside, you are greeted with a white, airy interior with bare brick columns, medieval frescoes and some Renaissance furniture, including the pulpit, organ and altar. Before the Reformation in 1536, the nave would have been empty of pews or pulpit; instead there were 75 side chapels where mass was said daily for the souls of the dead. On your left, on the wall to the left of the west window, don't miss the **mechanical clock** with figures of St George and the Dragon that re-enact the dragon's defeat and death cries on the hour.

The frescoes in the **Chapel of the Magi** on the south side are some of the best and date from 1462; they show Christ, various saints and Judgement Day. Opposite, on the north side, are **St Birgitte's Chapel** and **St Andrew's Chapel**, dating from 1511. The latter contains a large image of the death of John the Baptist; the former depicts the fathers of the church (Augustine, Hieronymus, Gregory and Ambrosius), along with several other saints, including St Birgitte sitting on a

Roskilde Rocks
Inspired by Woodstock in 1969, Roskilde has held an annual festival since 1970 (www.roskilde festival.dk). It ranks alongside Glastonbury in the rock calendar and has featured international and local artists such as Blur, Björk, the Scissor Sisters, Fat Boy Slim and rock legends Bob Dylan and Nirvana.

Devil May Care
Look out for the small green devil in Sankt Birgitte's Chapel who, armed with pen and ink, is writing down the names of anyone who is misbehaving.

dragon with St Lucius, the cathedral's patron saint.

The oldest frescoes are found at the east (altar) end and were part of the pre-Reformation, Catholic side chapels. On the north side of the **ambulatory**, note the fresco depicting Bishop Absalon and a little further to the south, the tomb of the three-legged 'ghost horse', said to be jet black with blazing red eyes, the sight of which was an omen of one's impending demise.

The **choir** has an ornate Renaissance altar piece that features scenes from the New Testament. Also here is the tomb of Denmark's first (and only other) queen, Margrethe I, and beautiful stalls carved with scenes from the Old Testament on the south side and New Testament on the north, with odd little trolls wandering through the narrative.

TO THE VIKING MUSEUM

Coming out of the cathedral, turn right, looking towards the sea. Cross Skolegade and head into leafy Lille Maglekildestræde. This takes you past the **Maglekilde** ❼ (Large Spring), on your right, and under a wooden well house that dates from 1927; note, here, the mermaid weathervane, from 1842. In the 19th century, this spring supplied water for five mills in industrialised Roskilde; it now yields one sixth of what it used to.

At the end of the road, turn right onto Maglekildevej, where you'll see a spring with water gushing out of the mouth of a head of Neptune. Walk past the **Roskilde Galleriet**, a com-

mercial art gallery, until you reach Sankt Claravej, lined with 17th-century cottages. Turn right and first left on to Havnevej and then left again onto Uglebjergvej.

St Jorgensberg's Church

At the junction, turn right onto Asyl-gade, which then turns into the pretty Kirkegade, with **St Jorgensbjerg Church** ❽ (Sankt Jorgensbjerg Kirke; July–mid-Aug: Mon–Fri 10am–noon; www.sjk.dk; free) on your right.

This is Denmark's oldest preserved stone church, with a choir and nave dating from the 11th century. Pop in if it is open; inside, there is a 19th-century votive ship model, a 16th-century crucifix and pulpit, and two bells in the tower dating from 1435 and 1597.

Walk through the churchyard, looking out over the lovely view of the fjord, and then down the hill until you come out on Havnevej. Turn left and head down to the **Viking Museum** standing on your right.

Above from far left: the cathedral's Gothic chapel and royal tombs, which mark out Danish history through the graves of generations of monarchs; reflecting outside the cathedral.

Shorter Route
If you want to save time, follow the signs from Skolegade for a more direct route to the Viking Museum.

Below: picturesque Lille Maglekildestræde.

Harbour Picnic
Roskilde's peaceful harbour is filled with white sails. There are several benches, and it's a nice place for a picnic, although there are also picnic tables in the museum if you prefer.

VIKING MUSEUM

Arguably the highlight of a trip to Roskilde is the excellent **Viking Museum** ❾ (Vikingeskibsmuseet; Roskilde Harbour; tel: 46 30 92 99; www.vikingeskibsmuseet.dk; daily 10am–5pm; charge).

Housed in a lovely waterside building, the museum and adjoining boatyards and workshops are dedicated to researching and recreating anything to do with Viking ships and sailing. The core exhibits are six boats that were discovered in 1962 in the channel close to Skuldelev, 20km (12 miles) north of Roskilde. They had been deliberately scuttled to create an underwater blockade against raiders. These boats have been restored in the boatyard, using tradional Viking methods and materials. The rest of the museum explores local Viking social and military history.

For lunch, there are two options, a restaurant boat, **MS Sagafjord**, see ⑪②, or the museum restaurant, **Snekken**, see ⑪③, near the entrance.

BACK TO TOWN

To take a different route back, turn left out of the museum. When you get to Strandengen, turn right and follow the road to the junction with Sankt Ibs Vej. **St James' Church** ❿ (Skt Ibs Kirke), a ruin with roots in the 12th century, stands on your right. Turn right and follow the road round until you come to **Roskilde Mini Town** ⓫ on your left, another millennium gift to the town in 1998. The model shows Roskilde as it was in the 14th century.

Cross the road and enter the **City Park** ⓬ (Byparken) through a gate on your left. Head left, right and then left (across the park, which is the site of various medieval archaeological remains), then cross the road to the cathedral. It is easy to see the variety of architectural styles from here. Don't forget to look back at the sea, with the ships' masts pointing skyward in the distance.

Walk round the cathedral into Domkirke Pladsen. If you haven't yet eaten, there is a nice little cellar restaurant, **Radhus Kaelderen**, see ⑪④, on the corner of Fordensbro.

Walk down Fordensbro into Stændertorvet, the main square, which was laid out as it is now in 1908. On your left stands the golden-walled **Roskilde Palace** ⓭ (Stændertorvet 3), a Baroque palace dating from the 1730s and built on the site of a medieval bishop's

Vikings Return to Dublin

The largest of the six Viking ships found in the fjord and now showcased in the Viking Museum is *Skuldelev 2*, a 30-m (100ft), ocean-going warship that was originally built in Dublin c.1040. She was reconstructed between 2000 and 2004 and, named

Havhingsten fra Glendalough (The Sea Stallion from Glendalough), set sail back to Dublin on 1 July 2007 with a crew of 70. She arrived, seven weeks and 1,852km (1,000 nautical miles) later, on 16 August.

palace. It is now home to: the **Museum of Contemporary Art** (tel: 46 36 88 74; Tue–Fri 11am–5pm; Sat–Sun noon–4pm), which hosts changing exhibitions; the **Palace Wing** (tel: 46 32 14 70; Tue–Sun noon–4pm), showcasing art exhibitions; and the **Palace Collections** (tel: 46 35 78 80; mid-May–mid-Sept: daily 11am–4pm; off-season Sat–Sun 2–4pm), a small museum that displays 17th- and 18th-century artefacts belonging to local merchants and townspeople.

On the right is the **Town Hall** ⑭, dating from 1884. Note its splendid tower, the only remaining part of the 12th-century church of St Laurentius, pulled down c.1550. The **ruins** (key held at the Borgerservice; Mon–Wed 10am–3pm, Thur 10am–5pm, Fri 10am–1pm, Sat 10am–noon; www.roskilde.dk) are preserved under the square.

BACK TO THE STATION

To return to the station, turn right out of the square down Skomagergade. Continue to the end and take a left down Blågårdsstræde. On the right is **Lützhøft Købmandsgård** ⑮ (Ringstedgade 6–8; Mon–Fri 11am–5pm, Sat 10am–2pm), an old merchant's house with a charming shop that is reminiscent of the 1920s, and the Museum of Tools, with a collection from the period 1840–1950.

Keep on until you reach Bredgade. Turn left and carry on, crossing Allehelgensgade on to Grønnegarde. Turn right into Fruegade. The **Church of Our Lady** stands on your right.

Dating from the late 11th century, the **Church of Our Lady** ⑯ (Vor Frue Kirke; tel: 46 35 58 14) was an important, wealthy church – so much so that St Margaret of Højelse, a relative of Bishop Absalon, was buried here in 1177. It was also connected to a Cistercian convent that was built close by in 1160. The convent was abolished in 1536, and its buildings and the eastern end of the church were demolished c.1600. It has a pretty whitewashed interior and the 17th-century pews were carved by Casper Luebbeke, Master of Roskilde.

Turn right out of the church and at the end, turn left onto Jernbanegade. The station is a little further along on your right.

Food and Drink 🍴

② MS SAGAFJORD
Roskilde Harbour; tel: 46 75 64 60; www.sagafjord.dk; Apr, Oct: Sat–Sun 1–3pm, Thur–Sun 6–9.30pm; May– Sept: daily 1–3pm, 6–9.30pm; €
Buffet or menu cruising in Viking waters along the Roskilde Fjord.

③ RESTAURANT SNEKKEN
Vindeboder 16; tel: 46 35 98 16; www.snekken.dk; 11.30am–10pm; €–€€
Café or restaurant meals in lovely, airy venue with views over the water.

④ RADHUS KAELDEREN
Fondensbro 1; tel: 46 36 01 00; www.raadhuskaelderen.dk; Mon–Sat 11am–11pm; €€
Good cellar restaurant with traditional Danish food. Seating in the small courtyard in summer.

Above from far left: reconstructions of Viking ships are used to take visitors for a trip on the fjord in the summer; Viking coins.

Shorter Route
For a shorter route to the station, cross Stændertorvet and walk down Allehelgensgade at the far left corner. Take the second left on to Grønnegarde and then turn right into Fruegade. Continue to the end and turn left onto Jernbanegade; the station is a little further along on your right.

Below: day trippers ready to explore Roskilde; one of six perfectly restored Viking ships.

HELSINGØR

Famous for its fictional association with William Shakespeare's Hamlet, Helsingør is a charming town on the banks of the Sound, just 6.5km (4 miles) away from Sweden aross the water.

Old Buildings

On Strandgade, look out for Nos 77–9, which date from 1577 and 1642 and the Court Building (1520) at Nos 72–4. The town hall, close to the cathedral, dates from 1855.

DISTANCE 3km (1¾ miles); further if visiting Technical Museum
TIME A half/full day
START Skibsklarerer gaarden
END Technical Museum
POINTS TO NOTE
You will need to do some careful planning to squeeze everything on this tour in. You may find it more convenient to do the tour in the opposite order.

Helsingør is an historic town, with entire streets of well-preserved, colourwashed buildings. For a flavour of the Old Town, cross the road from the station and walk down Broestræde. Turn

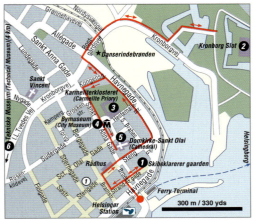

right and walk down Strandgade (Beach Street). Check out **Skibsklarerer gaarden ❶** (Strandgade 91; tel: 49 20 18 36; www.helsingor.dk/museum; Tue–Fri noon–4pm, Sat 10am–2pm; conducted tours every hour; charge), a former grocers and chandlers, originally dating from the 16th century. If you are ready for lunch, retrace your steps to Bramstræde and turn right to Stengade, the main pedestrian street, is parallel and is full of restaurants; check out **Madam Sprunck**, see ⑪①.

KRONBERG CASTLE

Walk down to Havnegade. Turn left and walk round the dock in the direction of the towers of **Kronborg Castle ❷** (Kronborg Slot; tel: 49 21 30 78; www.kronborgslot.dk; May–Sept: daily 10.30am–5pm, Oct: Tue–Sun 11am–4pm, Nov–Mar: Tue–Sun 11am–3pm, Apr: Tue–Sun 11am–4pm; charge). A Renaissance-style edifice, originally built in 1420, Kronberg was designed as a fortress to protect the town and to encourage trading ships to pay King Erik V the 'Sound Dues' that he demanded for sailing in these waters. It is famous as the model for Shakespeare's 'Elsinore' in *Hamlet*. It has a massive banqueting hall and some suitably miserable dungeons and is well worth a visit.

SANKT ANNA GADE

Head back onto Havnegade, taking a right up Kongensgade and then first left in Sankt Anna Gade, an ancient street of much historical interest.

Carmelite Priory and City Museum
The first place you come to, on your left, is the **Carmelite Priory ❸** (Karmeliterklosteret; Sankt Anna Gade 38; tel: 49 21 17 74; www.sctmariae.dk; mid-May–mid-Sept: daily 10am–3pm, mid-Sept–mid-May: daily 10am–2pm), a fine building dating from the mid-15th century. Its church (St Maria's/Sankt Maria Kirke) is decorated with recently restored frescoes dating from 1480–90, and the splendid Baroque organ dates from 1662–3.

Next door, in another priory building erected in 1516 as a sailors' hospital, the **City Museum ❹** (Bymuseum; Sankt Anna Gade 36; tel: 49 28 18 00; www.helsingordk/museum; daily noon–4pm; charge) has an interesting history, a Renaissance banqueting hall on the first floor and a mix of exhibits.

The Cathedral
Continue down the street and one block on on the same side you will see Helsingor's recently renovated red-brick **cathedral ❺** (Helsingør Domkirke; Sankt Anna Gade 12; tel: 49 21 04 43; www.helsingordomkirke.dk; May–Aug: 10am–4pm, Sept–Apr: 10am–2pm).

Originally a small Romanesque church dating from about 1200, this was the first church in Helsingør.

The current building dates from 1559 and was made a cathedral in 1961. It contains many monuments to the town's distinguished ancestors. Note particularly a 15th-century crucifix, the Renaissance pulpit of 1568 and the exuberantly carved wooden altarpiece, decorated with gold leaf.

Technical Museum
It's worth heading to the far end of town for the **Technical Museum ❻** (Danmarks Tekniske Museum; Fabriksvej 25; tel: 49 22 26 11; www.tekniskmuseum.dk; Tue–Sun 10am–5pm; also on Mon, 21 Jun–2 Aug only; charge), which is full of captivating vehicles, gadgets and appliances, including more than 30 aeroplanes, some of which belonged to Jacob Ellehammer (1871–1946), who designed and flew his own aeroplane in 1906, making him the 'second' European (after the Wright brothers, in 1903) ever to have flown.

To reach the museum from Helsingør station, catch bus No. 805 in the direction of Espergærde and ask the bus driver to stop at Fabriksvej; the stop is right outside the museum.

Food and Drink 🍴

① **MADAM SPRUNCK**
Stengade 48F; tel: 49 26 48 49; daily 11.30am–midnight; €–€€
This charming café-restaurant is housed in a half-timbered building dating from 1781. Light Danish and international meals are on offer during the day, with more expensive fare in the evening. You can eat out in the courtyard in summer.

Above from far left: spectacular Kronborg Castle inspired Shakespeare no less; typical colour-washed houses; castle detail.

Experimentarium
If you have time, visit the Experimentarium (Tuborg Havnevej 7, DK-2900 Hellerup; tel: 39 27 33 33; www.experimentarium.dk; Mon, Wed–Fri 9.30am–5pm, Tue 9.30am–9pm, Sat–Sun and holidays 11am–5pm; charge, 0–2s free), an interactive science centre that is great fun for kids. Get off the S train to/from Helsingør at Hellerup and take bus 1A or 21 from Hellerup Station.

ART TOUR

There are three world-class art galleries outside Copenhagen that it would be a pity to miss. With time, planning and a willingness to walk, you can combine two of them in one trip.

DISTANCE n/a
TIME A full day
START Ørdrupsgaard
END Louisiana
POINTS TO NOTE

These are not the easiest places to combine as public transport isn't direct but if you time it properly, you should make reasonable time. Try to do the trip Tue–Fri if you can, as Louisiana stays open then until 11pm. If you want to check timetables and routes, visit http://www.rejseplanen.dk.

Other Options

Depending on your timing, there are other places in Klampenborg to visit, namely Bellevue Beach (just out of the station on the side that you arrive on) and Dyrehaven, the old deer park, which is home to Bakken (www.bakken.dk; end Mar–Sept), the world's oldest funfair, reportedly on this site since the 16th century. If you decide to forgo Louisiana, the Aquarium (Akvarium; Kavalergården 1; tel: 39 62 32 83; www.akvarium.dk; Nov–Jan: 10am–4pm, Feb–Apr: 10am–5pm, May–Aug: 10am–6pm, Sept–Oct: 10am–5pm; charge) is not too far from Ørdrupsgaard; to reach it, turn left up Jaegersborg Allé or take bus No. 88.

Food and Drink 🍴

① LAVENDELHUSET
Ørdrupgaard; tel: 39 30 05 02; Tue, Thur–Fri noon–5pm, Wed 11am–6pm, Sat–Sun 11am–5pm; www.lavendelhusetordrupgaard.dk; €–€€
Housed in the new extension, this lovely glass-walled café looks out on the garden on both sides. The food, by Paul Cunningham, is very good; check out the à la carte menu online.

② LOUISIANA CAFE
Gammel Strandvej 13; Tue–Fri 11am–9.30pm, Sat–Sun 11am–4.30pm; €–€€
Sit by the fire in winter or by the water in summer in this very pleasant café. The food ranges from snacks and sandwiches to hot and cold dishes that change regularly.

ØRDRUPGAARD

Just 8km (5 miles) out of Copenhagen, this is perhaps the only trip when a car would be handy. Otherwise, put your walking boots on. The best way to **Ørdrupgaard ①** (Vilvordevej 110, Charlottenlund; tel: 39 64 11 83; www.ordrupgaard.dk; Tue and Thur–Fri 1–5pm; Wed 10am–6pm; Sat–Sun 11am–5pm; charge) is to take the S-Tog (direction Helsingør, 15 mins) to Ordrup Station and then to walk the remaining 2km (1 mile) along Hegels-vej. Alternatively, go to Klampenborg and take the No. 88 bus, but check the timetable, as there are only two every

hour. Or you can walk. Go down the stairs from the platform and turn left out of the station (not on the beach side) and follow the road round through some nice residential areas. Turn right at Dyrehavn bakket and follow the road to the lights and a sign to Lyngby 4 and a signal left to Charlottenlund. Turn left, the museum is a short way down on your left.

Ørdrupgaard is a lovely old house with a striking modern extension, full of Danish and European Impressionist paintings, with lots of premier-league artists, including Cézanne, Degas, Manet and Monet. There is also a delightful collection of paintings by Danish artist Vilhelm Hammershøi. Allow yourself plenty of time to tour the collection, as the free audio guide is thorough, and there is a pretty garden and excellent **café**, see ⑪①, supplied by the gourmet restaurant, **The Paul** (see p.74).

LOUISIANA

Walk (or take the No. 88 bus) to Klampenborg station (you can stay on the 88 bus to Louisiana but it will take about 1.5 hours). From here, take an S-Tog to Humlebaek (direction Helsingør); these run regularly. The journey takes about 30 minutes, and then it's a 20-minute, signposted walk.

The wonderful **Louisiana Modern Art Museum** ❷ (Gammel Strandvej 13, Humlebaek; tel: 49 10 07 19; www.louisiana.dk; Tue–Fri 11am–10pm, Sat–Sun 11am–6pm; charge) is housed in a building with numerous glass walls, so much of the time you will find yourself as aware of the gardens and water outside as you are of the art inside. The impressive collection features work by artists including Arp, Francis Bacon, Calder, Dubuffet, Max Ernst, Sam Francis, Giacometti, Kiefer, Henry Moore, Picasso, and Warhol. Giacometti's marvellous collection of 13 elongated figures is a highlight. The excellent **café**, see ⑪②, overlooking the Sound (sit outside in summer) is another incentive for making the trip and is a good place to have supper.

Arken

On the Baltic Coast is the **Arken Modern Art Museum** ❸ (Arken Museet for Moderne Kunst; Skovej 100, Ishøj; tel: 43 54 02 22; for special tours tel: 43 57 34 55; Thur–Tue 10am–5pm, Wed 10am–9pm; free), a marvellous building in the shape of a ship's hull that provides an ideal setting for the avant-garde works of art displayed here. An extension has recently been added, allowing the museum to hang a permanent exhibition – which includes a room dedicated solely to Brit-Art heavyweight Damien Hirst – for the first time. Arken also has a good café overlooking the sea. To get there, take the S-tog to Ishø (direction Hundige st, 20 mins), and bus No. 28; or the signposted walk takes 30–40 minutes.

DIRECTORY

A user-friendly alphabetical listing of practical information, plus hand-picked hotels and restaurants, clearly organised by area, to suit all budgets and tastes.

A

AGE RESTRICTIONS

In Denmark, you must be 18 to purchase alcohol and drink in a bar but there is no legal drinking age for young people drinking elsewhere and you can buy alcohol legally from the age of 16. The minimum age for driving is 18.

B

BUSINESS HOURS

General **shopping hours** in Denmark are Mon–Thur 9.30/10am–5.30pm, Fri 9.30/10am–6/7pm; Sat 9.30/10am–noon/1–4pm. Bakeries, florists and souvenir shops are also open on Sundays. Other shops are allowed to open 26 Sundays a year – which is usually the first Sunday of the month. On the first Saturday of every month, shops often stay open until 5pm. In tourist areas in Copenhagen, weekend hours may be extended, especially in summer.

Museums are often open late one night a week and closed on Mondays. Some have longer opening hours on Wednesdays.

Banks are usually open Mon–Wed and Fri 9.30am–4pm; Thur 10am–6pm. They are closed on public holidays. If you are looking to exchange money out of usual hours, **Den Danske Bank** at Copenhagen airport is open 6am–10pm and **Forex** at Hovedbânegard is open between 8am and 9pm.

Office hours are usually Mon–Fri 9am–4/4.30pm.

C

CLIMATE

Copenhagen is on the same latitude as Moscow and Edinburgh. The winter months, December–February, are cold and windy and there are only five hours of daylight, which precludes lots of time outdoors but would encourage Danish *hygge* or cosiness. February is the coldest month with an average daytime temperature of 0°C (32°F), July the warmest at 16°C (62°F). Like much of Europe it has had warmer summers recently. In summer there are between 16 and 18 hours of daylight on a clear day.

CRIME AND SAFETY

Copenhagen is one of the least dangerous places you could visit. However, it's never a bad thing to secure your personal possessions and not to take any personal risks. If you are victim of a crime, the police are very efficient and if there are witnesses, ask for help.

Vesterbro: Halmtorvet 20; tel: 33 25 14 48

Politivagten: Copenhagen Central Station; tel: 33 15 38 01; daily 7am–midnight

CUSTOMS REGULATIONS

Visitors may bring a limited quantity of spirits, wine and tobacco into Denmark. Visitors arriving from EU countries can bring in 800 cigarettes (or 400 cigarillos or 200 cigars or 1kg of tobacco) and 10l

of spirits (or 20l of fortified wine); 90l of table wine, 110l of beer. Non-EU residents can bring in 1l of spirits (or 2l of sparkling fortified wine), 2l of table wine, 200 cigarettes (or 100 cigarillos, 50 cigars or 250g of tobacco). Food articles that are not vacuum-packed by the manufacturer cannot be brought into Denmark. Articles imported in commercial quantities and presents of a value of more than 1,350dkk are subject to customs duty. When bringing in a large quantity of cash (over 40,000dkk) visitors must carry a certificate confirming the legality of the source.

There is no limit within reason to the amount of alcohol or tobacco that citizens of EU countries can take out of the country. US citizens can take home $400 of goods before they are liable to pay duty.

When travelling between EU member countries, it is no longer possible to buy duty-free goods but tax-free shopping is possible in many shops in Copenhagen for non-EU visitors for a minimum purchase of 300dkk. Collect a Global refund Taxfree Cheque from the store when you buy your goods. Show this and the receipt when leaving the country and collect a stamp; **Global refund** (www.global refund.com) will refund 13–19 per cent of purchase on application.

D

DISABLED TRAVELLERS

The Danes are generally very thoughtful about customers' needs but not all hotels are suitable for disabled travellers. Contact the Tourist Board, **Wonderful Copenhagen**, for information on hotels, transport, museums and attractions that are accessible or look under Handicap Facilities in the press section on their website.

For wheelchair users travelling by regional train (including the airport) contact the **DSB Handicap service**. All metro stations have lifts and most buses have collapsible ramps for the middle doors and a call button. Many cinemas and theatres have hearing loops; make sure to call venues for details. Most taxis offer specialised transport, but you will need to book ahead; one of the largest companies is **3 x 35 taxi**.

3 x 35 taxi: tel: 35 59 35 35; vagtchef@ taxa4x35.dk
DSB Handicap Service: tel: 70 13 14 19; handicoest@dsb.dk
Wonderful Copenhagen: www.visit copenhagen.com/composite-1350.htm; Woco handicap facilities: www.visit copenhagen.com/composite-253.htm; see also www.visitdenmark.com (look for 'disabled travel' in the 'Denmark A–Z' section)

E

ELECTRICITY

220 volts AC (50 Hz) is the Danish standard. If you are travelling with electrical or electronic devices be sure to bring a two-pin continental adapter with you.

Hand Luggage Alert
Be aware that if you are travelling from the EU, the amount of 'liquid' that you are entitled to carry in your hand luggage is limited to 100ml, unless you have bought your items once you have gone through passport control. Alcohol, contact lens solution, makeup etc, is confiscated if it exceeds the specified amounts, even if a bottle is not full.

EMBASSIES AND CONSULATES

Australia: Dampfærgevej 26, 2nd Floor; tel: 70 26 36 76

Canada: Kristen Bernikowsgade 1; tel: 33 48 32 00

UK: Kastelsvej 36/38/40; tel: 35 44 52 00

USA: Dag Hammarskjölds Allé 24; tel: 33 41 71 00; after-hours emergencies: 35 55 92 70

For more information or addresses and information on other embassies, visit www.embassyworld.com/embassy/Denmark/Denmark2.html

EMERGENCY NUMBERS

Emergency services: 112

Copenhagen airport: 32 45 14 48

Politivagten (local police): 33 15 38 01

Doctor on call: 70 13 00 41

24-hour doctor watch: 38 88 60 41

AA breakdown: 88 00 25

G

GAY TRAVELLERS

Denmark doesn't bat an eyelid about gays and lesbians and has been pioneering acceptance and equal rights for decades. In 1989 it became the first country to recognise same-sex marriages and in 1999 it became legal for married gay people to adopt their partner's children. For advice and information, contact **The National Association of Gays and Lesbians** (Landsforeningen for Bøsser og Lesbiske), set up in 1948, or check out their website for up-to-date information on gay life and venues. To have dinner with local gay people, get in touch with **Meet Gay Copenhagen**.

The National Association of Gays and Lesbians: Telgårdstræde 13, Baghuset; tel: 33 13 19 48; www.lbl.dk, www.gayguide.dk

Meet Gay Copenhagen: tel: 27 21 80 65; www.meetgaycopenhagen.dk

H

HEALTH

Tourists are covered by public health services according to agreements between Denmark and their home country and, in an emergency, hospital treatment is mainly free to tourists of all nationalities. However, if the emergency is deemed to have occurred as a result of a pre-existing condition, costs for services received may be payable. Payment to pharmacies and doctors must be paid in full on the spot and refunds are obtainable from the nearest municipal or health insurance office before leaving Denmark. If you cannot do this or do not have the correct documentation, you need to contact the relevant authorities when you get home.

Visitors from a Schengen country (several EU countries plus Iceland, Norway and Switzerland), may bring in up to 30 days' supply of prescription drugs with them; visitors from non-Schengen countries may bring in 14 days' supply. Documentation regarding

Gay Travel Agency

Set up in 2006, Pink Viking is Denmark's first tour operator to offer inbound and outbound trips for gay and lesbian clients wishing to visit Scandinavia. For more information contact Pink Viking; tel: +45 61 79 74 65; www.pinkviking.net

the necessity of the remedy may be required upon entry if you come from a non-Schengen country. EU nationals should carry their European Health Insurance card.

Pharmacies are designated by a green 'A' for Apotek. Credit cards are not accepted in pharmacies. Full payment is required for all medications. **Late-night opening**: Steno Apotek (24 hours); Vesterbrogade 6C (opposite main station); tel: 33 14 82 66

LOCALS

Apart from chatting in bars and clubs, if you would like to meet the locals in the comfort of their homes, contact **Meet the Danes** for reasonably priced, traditional home-hosted dinners. They try to pair up guests and hosts in relation to age as well as interests.
Meet the Danes: www.meetthedanes. dk; info@meetthedanes.dk

LOST PROPERTY

For items lost on the bus or local (S) train, contact Lyshøjgårdsvej 80, Valby; tel: 35 53 00 09. For all other losses, ring the police station at Slotsherrensvej 113; tel: 38 74 88 22.

MAPS

The tourist board and most hotels offer free city maps with sights marked

on them. Some also show bus routes. These are fine for sightseeing. If you need a street index, the Insight Copenhagen Fleximap is a good option.

MEDIA

Newspapers: Most of the major English-language newspapers are readily available and there are also over 100 fashion and lifestyle magazines in English. For local news in English get the weekly *Copenhagen Post* (free, usually available in hotel lobbies, tourist information and some other public places). The national newspapers of Denmark are *Aktuelt*, *Borsen*, *Ekstra Bladet*, *Jyllands-Posten* and *Politiken*.

Television: Cable and satellite television is widely available so it's easy to get access to channels in English and other foreign languages. Foreign films are rarely dubbed into Danish and appear in the original version with subtitles. Radio Denmark International (1062 Mz) offers international news in English at 10.30am, 5.05pm and 10pm.

MONEY

Cash machines: ATMs are open 24 hours and can usually be found outside banks and metro stations.

Credit cards: Credit cards are accepted in many places but they will usually attract an additional fee. Many smaller, independent retailers, including pharmacies, however, do not accept them so do not rely on plastic.

Above from far left: celebrating at the Mermaid Pride; meet the Danes; Copenhagen on the map; Thotts Palace houses the French Embassy.

Budget Copenhagen
If you visit in summer, there are several ways to keep the cost down. Much of Copenhagen is accessible on foot, parks are free, there are quite often free entertainments (see www.visit copenhagen.dk). The National Theatre (already much subsidised) sells reduced unsold tickets on the day from 4pm and if you book a hotel (even a posh one) ahead of time you are more likely to get a reduced deal.

Currency: Denmark still eschews the euro. Danish notes come in 1,000dkk, 500dkk, 200dkk, 100dkk and 50dkk. Coins are in denominations of 20dkk, 10dkk, 5dkk 2dkk, 1dkk, 50 øre (half a krone) and 25 øre. At the time of writing there are roughly 10dkk to £1 sterling.

P

POST

Post offices are usually open Mon–Fri 9/10am–5/6pm, Sat (if open) 9/10am–noon/2pm. The post office at Hoved-banegård (Central Station) has longer opening hours. Poste Restante mail can be collected from all Danish post offices. 'A-mail' or Prioritaire mail is the fastest international option.

Hovedbanegård: Mon–Fri 8am–9pm, Sat 9am–4pm, Sun (and public holidays) 10am–4pm; www.postdanmark.dk.

R

RELIGION

Denmark's Constitution provides for freedom of religion. The evangelical Lutheran church is the State church and enjoys some privileges not available to other faiths, including government funding. In January 2002, 84.3 per cent of Danes belonged to the Lutheran church. The second largest religious community (three per cent of the population) is Muslim, followed by the Catholic Church, Jehovah's Witnesses, Baptists, Pentecostals, Mormons and

Jews. Approximately nine per cent of the citizens are without a religion.

Places of Worship
Catholic: Sakramentskirken, Nørre-brogade 27C; tel: 31 35 68 25; Sun 10am (Danish), 6pm (English), Tue, Thur–Fri 11am (Danish), Wed 5pm (English), Sat 5pm (Danish), Sep-Jun: Sat 6.15pm (French).
Church of England: St Albans, Churchill Parken 6, Langelinie; tel: 39 62 77 36; www.st-albans.dk; services (all in English): Sun 9am (Holy Com-munion), 10.30am (Sung Eucharist), Wed 10.30am (Holy Communion).
Jewish: Copenhagen Synagogue, Krystalgade 12, tel: 33 12 88 68; only open during services: Mon, Thur 6.45am, Tue–Wed, Fri 7am, Sat 9am; daily at sunset.
Muslim: Al-Tauba Mosque, Vester-brogade 80B; tel: 31 21 18 96; services: Fri 1.30pm.

S

SMOKING

A smoking ban in public indoor places came into force in August 2007. This includes public buildings and private business; including restaurants, pubs, shops, public transport, entertainment venues and workplaces. Small (up to 40m²/430ft²) establishments that don't serve fresh food are exempt. Some places have installed special smoking rooms, otherwise, you must smoke outside. However, many places supply a heater and blanket or two if you need them.

Religious Harmony
Denmark has a long history of welcoming religious minorities and affording them equal treatment, although a recent increase in the Muslim population has led to some tensions. However, there is some question over whether these relate to religion or differences in language and ethnicity, and the latter may be at least as important in explaining unequal access to well-paying jobs and social advancement. The integration of immigrant groups from Islamic countries has become an important political and social topic of discussion.

TELEPHONES

Local Danish numbers have eight digits. There are no area codes.
Directory assistance: 113
International calls from Denmark: 00 + country code + area code + personal number
International calls to Denmark: 00 + 45 + personal number
International country codes: Britain +44, France +33, Germany +49, Ireland +353, Italy +39, Japan +81, Norway +47, Sweden +46, USA +1

Public telephones: These accept coins (but not the small copper ones), pre-paid telephone cards and some take credit cards. Lift the receiver and insert your card or coin. Insert 5–20dkk for international connections; change is not given regardless of whether you have been connected or not. Collect calls to the US are not possible.

TIME ZONES

Denmark is one hour ahead of GMT. Summer time, when the clocks go forward one hour, begins on the last Sunday in March and the clocks are not put back until the last Sunday in October.

TOURIST INFORMATION

The Wonderful Copenhagen tourist office is opposite the main station. You can get brochures, book hotels, drink coffee etc. Everyone speaks English. To get tourist info on your mobile, text 'woco' to +45 22 90 40 04 and a link will be sent to you or use mobil.woco.dk, which will connect you direct to the guide. The service is free although you will have to pay the usual mobile rate.

Wonderful Copenhagen Tourist Information: Bernstorffsgade 1; tel: 70 22 24 42; www.visitcopenhagen.com; www.visitdenmark.dk; touristinfo@woco.dk; Mon–Fri 9am–4pm, Sat 9am–2pm.

Listings: There are no listing magazines but the *Copenhagen Post*, the English weekly newspaper, has a useful weekly guide to what's on, which comes out on Fridays. For Danish speakers, there are guide sections on Friday in *Politiken* and *Berlingske*, and the free monthly paper *Citadel*.

TRANSPORT

Getting to Copenhagen is easy, with many airlines offering daily flights, as well as direct rail services from Sweden and Germany. Access from the airport is also very straightforward with train, bus and taxi options, which will take you to the city centre. Prices were correct at the time of going to press. There are also ferry services to Copenhagen *(see p.106)*.

Getting There
By plane: Copenhagen Airport, Kastrup (www.cph.dk) lies 12km (7.5 miles) east of the city centre, on Amager Island. A **rail shuttle service** links the airport and Hovedbanegård, Copenhagen's Central Station. The fast train

Tour Operators
There are plenty of tour operators in Copenhagen offering tours, walks, bus and bike rides, ghost walks and all manner of information. Contact Wonderful Copenhagen or visit their offices for more information.

link leaves from Track *(Spor)* 2 (located beneath Terminal 3, where all passengers go for baggage reclaim and customs), three times every hour; the journey takes about 12 minutes and costs about 27dkk. Ticket sales close at 11pm.

An **airport bus service** runs every 15 minutes to Hovedbanegård (Central Station). It takes 25 minutes and costs about 35dkk, which is slightly more expensive than the train.

Local buses (Nos. 250S, 12, 96N) also travel to the city and leave from outside Terminals 1 and 3 every 15 minutes between 5.30am and midnight. They take 35 minutes (a bit longer than the airport bus, but less than half the price, at 16.50dkk).

There is a **taxi rank** at Terminal 3. A taxi to the centre will cost between about 170–220dkk depending on the time and includes VAT and tip.

To minimise your environmental impact, you can measure your travel usage and gain carbon emission credits. Visit www.carbonresponsible.com and www.climatecare.org for details.

By train: Trains arrive daily from Germany, Britain and Sweden arriving at Hovedbanegård opposite Tivoli and the tourist office. The S-tog (local) trains also leave from the Central Station and run on a separate network.

For European rail enquiries and bookings, contact **German Railways**: tel: +44 0870 243 5363; http://reiseauskunft.bahn.de

For Danish and outgoing international rail enquiries and bookings, contact **Danish Rail** (DSB): tel: 70 13 14 15; www.dsb.dk; salginfo@dsb.dk for train tickets in Denmark; and tlf salgudland@dsb.dk for international train journeys.

By bus: For coach travel to Denmark, contact Eurolines UK, tel: 0870 514 3219; www.eurolines.com. For coach travel from Denmark, contact Eurolines Scandinavia, tel: +45 70 10 00 30. The buses stop at Copenhagen's Central Station. Buses for onward journeys leave either from outside the station or nearby Rådhuspladsen.

By ferry: There are several options for arriving by sea although only ferries from Poland, Sweden and Norway arrive in Copenhagen itself. The Swedish ferries have been seriously affected by the opening of the Øresund bridge, which gives direct rail and road access to Mälmo in Sweden. Most ferries operate from the new ferry terminal in Copenhagen, north of the cruise-ship harbour, close to Nordhavn train station. Ferries from the UK arrive at Esbjerg on Jutland three hours' drive away and from Germany at Rødby, Rønne and Gedser.

For ferries to and from the UK (19 hrs) and Norway (16 hrs), contact **DFDS Seaways**; www.dfds.co.uk; tel: 0871 522 9955 (UK); tel: +45 33 42 30 00 (Oslo); tel: +45 33 42 30 00 (Copenhagen).

For ferries to and from Poland (12 hrs), contact **Polferries** (Swinoujscie): tel: +45 33 13 52 23.

For ferries to and from Germany (1–2 hrs), contact **Scandlines**; tel: + 45 33 15

15 15 (Denmark) or +49 (0) 18 05/11 66 88 (Gemany); www.scandlines.de

For the **Port of Copenhagen** contact PO Box 2083, Ndr. Toldbod 7, DK-1013 Copenhagen K; tel: +45 33 47 99 99; www.cphport.dk

By car: Most British visitors arrive by ferry either direct from Harwich in the UK to Esbjerg or from Puttgarden in Germany to Rødby. Then take the E20 from Esbjerg and the E47 from Rødby.

Both the Storebælt bridge/tunnel from Funen to Sjælland, and the Øresund bridge from Malmö to Copenhagen levy a toll.

Danish roads are in good condition and signs are easy to follow. Speed limits in towns are in general 50kmh (30mph), on A roads 80kmh (50mph) and on motorways 110–130kmh (68–80mph). The Danes generally keep to these restrictions. If you are caught speeding, you will be fined on the spot.

Getting Around

Local transport tickets: For fare purposes, the city is divided into zones. Fares are charged on the number of zones that you pass through (minimum two); the most expensive zone determines the cost of your journey. You must show your ticket if asked to do so by an inspector.

The bus, metro and S-tog (local train) all use the same tickets so you can change between them without buying a new one. The cheapest option is to buy a discount Clip Card of 10 tickets, which can be shared between several people if you wish. Alternatively, if you

have a Copenhagen Card *(see margin)*, local travel is free. Tickets can be bought on the bus, at ticket offices or vending machines at stations and at the bus terminus at Rådhuspladsen. Discount cards, with an average saving of 40 per cent cannot be bought on the bus.

Individual tickets have a time limit of an hour for two zones (adult 19dkk/ child 9.50dkk) and you must clip your ticket when you get on the bus or on the train platform before you get on.

Using the night bus or the metro between 1am and 5am costs double the daytime fare.

By bus: You can take a bus to practically anywhere although everything is so close in the centre that you'll find it's usually easier to walk. Buses are regular and nearly all of them stop at either Rådhuspladsen or Hovedbanegård (Central Station).

Buses run daily between 5am and 12.30am and there are additional night buses from Rådhuspladsen (City Hall Square) to the suburbs.

Buses are yellow and you get on at the front and off at the back.

By S-tog: The S-tog (local train) connects Copenhagen with other towns on Sjælland. In the city, it runs underground. Tickets are available at all S-tog stations.

By metro: The metro (tel: 70 15 16 15; www.m.dk) operates daily from 5am until midnight and from Thur–Sun, it is open 24 hours. Trains run every 3–6 minutes. There are two lines, M1

Copenhagen Card

A Copenhagen Card (CPH Card) gives entry to 60 attractions in the Copenhagen area, offers some discounts and also entitles you to free travel on trains and buses. They are valid for 24 hours (199dkk for adults/ 129dkk for children) or 72 hours (429dkk/249dkk). Up to two children under the age of 10 are allowed free with each adult card. You can buy them online or at the tourist office.

runs from Vanløse Station to Copen-hagen Airport in East Amager, and M2 runs from Vanløse Station to Ørestad in West Amager. Both lines take you through the heart of the city.

Although the trains are driverless and fully automatic, there are stewards on the train. In addition, all trains and stations are equipped with CCTV.

Metro customer service: tel: 70 15 16 15 (Mon–Fri 8am–6pm); www.m.dk; **Bus and metro planner**: www.dsb.dk/journey_planner

By bicycle: The Danes are avid cyclists; bicycles enjoy equal status with cars on Copenhagen's roads, and consequently they usually make rapid and relatively safe progress. When using the cycleways, keep to the right and you must always use lights at night or risk an instant 500dkk fine.

As a visitor, you can still access a bike either by hiring one or, in summer (Apr–Nov), using one of Copenhagen's **City Bikes** (www.bycyklen.dk), which are available at 110 stands around the inner city. Cyclists put a 20-dkk coin into a slot to unlock a bike, and can keep it for as long as they like. When the bike is returned to a stand, the money is refunded. The bikes may only be used within the old ramparts of the city, but this is where the sights are.

Pick up a City Bike Map from the Tourist Information Office located at Vesterbrogade 4A, right opposite the entrance to Tivoli. Alternatively, go on a guided bike tour and everything will be provided.

Bike rental varies from 60–75dkk per day; 105–135dkk for two days; 150–190dkk for three days. Deposits are 200–500dkk. Try:
City Safari (bike tours), Strandgade 27B, Christianshavn; tel: 33 23 94 90; www.citysafari.dk
Kobenhavns Cykelbørs, Gothers-gade 157; tel: 33 14 07 17; Mon–Fri 8.30am–5.30pm; Sat 10am–1pm; www.cykelboersen.dk
Kobenhavns Cykler, Reventlowsgade 11 (behind the main station); tel: 33 33 86 13; Mon–Fri 8am–5.30pm, Sat 9am–1pm); www.copenhagen-bikes.dk
Østerport Cycler, Oslo Plads 9; tel 33 33 85 13; Mon–Fri 8am–6pm, Sat 8am–1pm; www.oesterport-cykler.dk

Harbour buses: There are two harbour buses, Nos. 901 and 902, which run daily from 6am–6/7pm, every 10 min-utes between Den Sorte Diamant near Slotsholmen and *Gefionspringvandet* near *The Little Mermaid*, zigzagging between the two shores. The complete journey takes 20 mins and costs 30dkk for adults and 25dkk for children. Clip Cards and Copenhagen Cards can also be used. There is a suggestion that these may not be retained but no deci-sion had been made at time of printing.

By car: Don't bother; the Danes don't, it's more eco-friendly not to and it's really not practical. You will be surprised at how few cars there are on the road and how many bikes! But if you do hire a car, you must be over 20 years old and hold a valid licence. Some car firms may stipulate that you have to be over 25.

Danes drive on the right and speed limits are 110 or 130 kmh (66 or 80 mph) on motorways, 80 kmh (50 mph) on other roads and 50 kmh (30 mph) in a built-up area. Take a UK or EU driving licence and a warning triangle, and wear a seat belt at all times.

Headlights must be dipped at all times. Be aware of cycle lanes on both sides of the road in towns. *Parkering Forbudt* means No Parking. For information see www.parking.dk.

Car hire companies

Europcar: tel: 0845 758 5375, www.europcar.com

Hertz: tel: 0870 844 8844, www.hertz.com

By taxi and rickshaw: Taxis can be identified by the sign on the roof with the word FRI, meaning 'free'. Most drivers speak English and often some German. They can give you receipts and you can pay with a credit card. The basic fare for a taxi is 19dkk, then 11dkk for each km thereafter Mon–Fri 7am–4pm; 14dkk per km Fri–Sat 11pm–7am and 12.1dkk per km at all other times. Tips are not expected (a service charge is included in the fare), but it is usual to round up the final amount.

Cycle rickshaws are also available for short rides around town and can be found at Storkspringvandet, Nyhavn, Tivoli and Rådhuspladsen. Prices vary so negotiate first.

Amager Øbro taxi: tel: 32 51 51 51
Copenhagen Rickshaw: tel: 35 43 01 22; www.rickshaw.dk

Hovedstadens taxi: tel: 38 77 77 77
Kobenhavns Taxa: tel: 35 35 35 35
Minibuses/handicap: tel: 35 39 35 35
Taxa-motor: tel: 38 10 10 10

By Foot: Copenhagen is an ideal city to explore on foot. It is very compact, with a well-preserved Old Town with winding cobbled streets, stuccoed houses and a network of canals, and almost everything is easily accessible by foot. Despite the fact that the reliable public transport system is superb, walking around Copenhagen is the best way to discover this city's inestimable charms. However, if you are heading over to Nørrebro or down to Frederiksberg, it's worth hopping on a bus.

VISAS

Citizens of the EU do not need a visa; other visitors should check with their country. Visitors not obliged to have a visa are allowed to stay in Denmark for up to 90 days. If you wish to work, all foreign nationals are usually required to have a work and residence permit as a prerequisite to seeking paid or unpaid work in Denmark. See www.nyidanmark.dk/en-us/coming_to_dk/coming_to_dk.htm.

WEIGHTS AND MEASURES

The metric system is used in Denmark, as in all of continental Europe.

Above from far left: going underground; Copenhagen is relatively car-free; danger; do like the locals and get on your bike.

ACCOMMODATION

Cab Inn City

Mitchellsgade 14; tel: 33 46
16 16; www.cabinn.dk; S-tog:
Hovedbanegård; €

There are three of these attractive,
functional budget hotels in Copenhagen *(see p.115 for the other two)*.
Their decor is modern Danish, space
is used effectively (many rooms have
bunk beds – think of a ship's cabin,
hence 'cabinn') and the all-inclusive
breakfasts (50dkk) are healthy, copious
and good value. A good option for
families and anyone not expecting to
do much more than sleep here. This
particular hotel is only a short walk
from buzzing Tivoli.

Danhostel Copenhagen City

H.C. Andersens Boulevard 50;
tel: 33 11 85 85; www.danhostel.dk/
copenhagencity; bus: 33; €

A five-star youth hostel with a great
location right in the centre of town
and far-reaching views. It's modern,
comfortable and has plenty of family
rooms (accommodating up to 6 people),
which are extremely good value if you
fill them up. You will need an international YHA card but the investment
is covered by the saving on the cost
of a bed.

Hotel Alexandra

H.C. Andersens Boulevard 8; tel: 33
74 44 44; www.hotel-alexandra.dk;
bus: 33; €€€€

Formerly an apartment block dating
from the 1880s, this lovely hotel has
been in business since 1910. It is
stylishly decorated with plenty of
20th-century classics, from Arne
Jacobsen furniture (see room 223 in
particular) to Kaare Klint chairs and
Poul Henningsen lighting and has
gained 'The Green Key', a certificate
given to hotels that pay special atten-
tion to the environment and to health.
Definitely one of Copenhagen's nicer
hotels (of which there are many).

Hotel Astoria

Banegårdspladsen 4; tel: 33 29 80
70; www.dgi-byen.com; S-tog:
Hovedbanegård; €€

This old railway hotel dating from
the 1930s has been renovated,
keeping elements of the 1930s original (including the revolving doors
at the entrance, the first in Denmark), while updating the rooms to
suit more modern tastes and require-
ments. The rooms are designed in
black and white with shades of grey
and purple as contrasting colours and
the furniture is modern. As a new
member of the dgi-Byen group,
guests also have access to the swim
centre and spa a short walk away.
Depending on when you visit, there
may be noise from the building works
being done in front of the station.

Price for a standard double room for one night without breakfast in high season:	
€€€€	over 1,600dkk
€€€	1,400–1,600dkk
€€	1,000–1,400dkk
€	under 1,000dkk

Hotel Danmark

Vester Voldgade 89; tel: 33 11 48 06; www.hotel-danmark.dk; bus: 6a, 12, 26, 29, 33; €€

Located next to Rådhuspladsen, this modern, bright hotel offers rooms tastefully furnished in subdued Scandinavian style. Underground parking is available.

Hotel Fox

Jarmers Plads 3; tel: 33 13 30 00; www.hotelfox.dk; bus: 2a, 5a, 14, 66, 67, 68, 173e, 250S; €€–€€€€

A short walk from Rådhuspladsen, this is definitely one of Copenhagen's most extreme hotels – it's either your cup of tea, or it isn't. All the rooms have been individually designed by 21 international artists and vary from startling white to crimson, green and fully-tiled. Make sure to check out rooms on the web before you check in as you can't change rooms once you get there; also note, though, that while the hotel will do its best to give you the room you want, there are no guarantees. The bar and restaurant downstairs are good.

Hotel Kong Frederik

Vester Voldgade 25; tel: 33 12 59 02; www.remmen.dk; bus: 6a, 12, 26, 29, 33; €€€€

Although named in 1898, the history of this site as a hotel and inn dates back to the 14th century. Situated close to Rådhuspladsen and Tivoli, the hotel's recent renovation has retained its classic English atmosphere.

Imperial Hotel

Vester Farimagsgade 9; tel: 33 12 80 00; www.imperialhotel.dk; bus: 12, 40; €€€

A good location next to Vesterport Station and a few minutes' walk from Rådhuspladsen and Tivoli Gardens, this modern, stylish hotel is far more prepossessing on the inside than on the outside, with well-appointed, elegant rooms, as well as fine restaurants and on-site parking.

Le Méridien Palace Hotel

Rådhuspladsen 57; tel: 33 14 40 50; www.palacehotel.dk; bus: all Rådhuspladsen buses; €€€–€€€€

An imposing historical landmark on Rådhuspladsen with its own rival clocktower, the Palace has been newly renovated and now boasts five stars. The public areas thankfully retain their old-world, Victorian grandeur while the bedrooms, which are all a good size, especially for Copenhagen, have been stylishly redesigned using a modern idiom.

Radisson SAS Royal Hotel

Hammerichsgade 1; tel: 33 42 60 00; www.radissonsas.com; bus: 6a, 26, S-tog: Vesterport, Hovedbanegård; €€€–€€€€

This is Copenhagen's most iconic hotel; designed, down to the cutlery and the door knobs, by the famous architect and designer, Arne Jacobsen. Although only one room (606) retains its original decor, this hotel is still popular with the rich and famous and has a nice retro/modern feel. There is also a popular restaurant,

Above from far left: every room is a feast for the eyes at Hotel Fox.

Where to Stay

Many hotels are near Hovenbanegård (Central Station), the cheaper ones are around the Vesterbro area and the more expensive ones around Rådhuspladsen, within a short walk of the city's main sights. There are also several smart hotels around Kongens Nytorv and Nyhavn, but don't always expect a view. A little bit out of the way, but with good views, are the new hotels on Kalvebod Brygge, south of Slotsholmen. Alternatively, head away from the tourist centre and stay near Rosenborg or Amalienborg, or even in the suburbs – they really are not very far away.

Breakfast

Many hotels include breakfast with the room; always ask as otherwise it usually costs between 1,000 and 1,700dkk. This may seem a lot but a coffee and pastry will set you back 600–700dkk in a café, so a hearty breakfast of all you can eat may well be a good investment.

Alberto K, on the top floor, with fabulous views over Tivoli Gardens and the city. Centrally located and just a short walk from Rådhuspladsen, Strøget and the University Quarter. There is also a sauna and private parking. Rates are generally lower at weekends and the family rooms can be quite reasonable if there are four of you.

Scandic Copenhagen

Vester Søgade 6; tel: 33 14 35 35; www.scandichotels.com/copenhagen; €€€

A comfortable, centrally placed, skyscraper hotel that looks out over Copenhagen's reservoirs and the Tycho Brahe Planetarium. It is popular with both business and leisure travellers (including families as it caters for tots to teens, see website for details) and can offer non-smoking floors, free internet, friendly staff and a recommended breakfast.

The Square

Rådhuspladsen 14; tel: 33 38 12 00; www.thesquarecopenhagen.com; bus: all Rådhuspladsen buses; €€€€

On the corner of Rådhuspladsen, this air-conditioned hotel, converted from an office block, may not be much to look at from the outside but on the inside offers several grades of stylishly decorated rooms. There is also a rooftop breakfast room offering a copious breakfast and wonderful views. Four years after it first opened in 2003, it won a World Travel Award in the category 'Denmark's Leading Bou-

tique Hotel'. Note that rooms looking over the square can be a bit noisy if you open the window onto the balcony.

Strøget and Around

Ascot Hotel

Studiestræde 61; tel: 33 12 60 00; www.ascot-hotel.dk; €€€€

Set in a distinguished old bathhouse building in the Latin Quarter, this pleasantly decorated hotel, with a mixture of antiques and modern furniture, also offers suites, some with kitchenettes if you are into a bit of self-catering. It's very central and you won't be bothered by traffic.

Hotel Kong Arthur

Nørre Søgade 11; tel: 33 11 12 12; www.kongarthur.dk; €€€€

Established in 1882 and situated slightly off the beaten track beside Peblinge Sø, this family-owned hotel has retained much of its original charm with attractive rooms and a pretty, conservatory-type inner courtyard. It is a popular choice with both Danish and foreign visitors and has a friendly and very Danish atmosphere. Some of the suites have jacuzzis. Treatments are available from the new Avalon spa located in the hotel.

Price for a standard double room for one night without breakfast in high season:

€€€€	over 1,600dkk
€€€	1,400–1,600dkk
€€	1,000–1,400dkk
€	under 1,000dkk

Hotel 27

Løngangstræde 27; tel: 70 27
56 27; www.hotel27.dk; bus: 6a;
€€–€€€

Stylishly decorated to Danish taste
using a palette of red, black and white,
this is a reasonably priced 'life style'
hotel in the centre of town. It is also
home to the new Absolut Icebar, a bar
entirely made of ice hailing from
Lapland, which serves vodka shots in
ice glasses (150dkk extra per person
for 45 mins).

Ibsens Hotel

Vendersgade 23; tel: 33 13 19 13;
www.ibsenshotel.dk; €€

In the same group as the Hotel Kong
Arthur and Hotel Fox, this is a pleasant,
comfortable three-star hotel, although
it won't win awards for striking decor.
Located between Nørreport Station
and Peblinge Sø, it is a 15-minute walk
from the city centre.

Sankt Petri

Krystalgade 22; tel: 33 45 91 00;
www.hotelsktpetri.com; €€€€

This upmarket, modern five-star hotel
is located in the ancient centre of the
town. 'Bespoke' is a word that applies
to virtually everything here; from the
original artworks on the walls to the
orchids and designer modern decor.
The bathrooms are stunning. There
is a good restaurant, a couple of excellent bars and a pretty atrium where
live jazz is played and international
DJs spin their discs. In summer, there
is also an attractive outdoor area for
drinks and dinner.

Best Western Hotel City

Peder Skramsgade 24; tel: 33 13 06
66; www.hotelcity.dk; €€

Located in an elegant town house, the
City has an international feel, clearly
expressed in its striking modern decor.
It has a hospitable and friendly atmosphere and there is access to tennis
courts if you feel the need for more
exercise after pounding the streets.

Copenhagen Strand

Havnegade 37; tel: 33 48 99 00;
www.copenhagenstrand.dk;
€€€–€€€€

Opened in 2000, this cosy three-star
hotel can be found on a side street just
off Nyhavn in a converted warehouse
dating from 1869. Its decor is slightly
rustic yet modern and brings to mind
its maritime position and history.

Hotel d'Angleterre

Kongens Nytorv 34; tel: 33 12 00
95; www.remmen.dk; bus: 1a, 15,
19, 26, 999, S-tog: Kongens Nytorv;
€€€€

The wealthy, the important and the
beautiful take refuge behind this
grand façade on Kongens Nytorv.
This is the place for old-fashioned
formal elegance and the only hotel in
Copenhagen where you will find a
Victorian palm court. But fear not,
the plumbing is up to scratch and
modern facilities, including a spa and
fitness centre with a 10x12m (33x40ft)
heated pool and a posh restaurant, are
all instantly available.

**Above from far
left:** the tranquil
inner courtyard at
Hotel Kong Arthur;
the rooms and
stylish bar in Hotel
27; indulge yourself
at the beautiful
Avalon spa inside
Hotel Kong Arthur.

Early Booking
Early bookings are
usually cheaper than
the official rack
rates; web bookings
are often cheaper
still and some hotels
have special deals.
However, it is always
worth ringing up to
find out if a hotel
(even the expensive
ones) can give you
an even better deal;
they may be able to
if business is slow.

Hotel Opera

Tordenskjoldsgade 15; tel: 33 47 83 00; www.hotelopera.dk; €€€

This is another charming three-star hotel belonging to the Arp-Hansen group. Located on a side street close to the Royal Theatre on Kongens Nytorv, this English-inspired hotel dates from 1869. Rooms are comfortable but vary in size, as do the beds. See the website for more information.

71 Nyhavn Hotel

Nyhavn 71; tel: 33 43 62 00; www. 71nyhavnhotel.com; €€€

This charming hotel overlooking the Sound is housed in two former warehouses on Nyhavn, which were once used to store spices from the Far East. The atmosphere is one of upmarket rusticity and many original features remain. The rooms are full of character but not overly large and some have harbour views. The restaurant is recommended.

Amalienborg and Around

Copenhagen Admiral Hotel

Tolbodgade 24–8; tel: 33 74 14 14; www.admiralhotel.dk; €€€–€€€€

A stone's throw from Nyhavn, this is another warehouse conversion (formerly a granary) full of original beams and a modern rustic stance with designer teak furniture; every room is different. Outside iron canons salute you as you pass into the enormous galley-like lobby with naval memorabilia and some lovely model ships on view. It features its own, very good restaurant, SALT, in partnership with Conran and a sauna and steam bath facility on the top floor.

Front Hotel

Skt Annæ Plads 21; tel: 33 13 34 00; www.front.dk; €€€€

One link in the sophisticated Remmen chain, this is a stylish, modern boutique hotel set in a quiet location not far from Nyhavn. Kids are welcome and some rooms have a stunning harbour view of the Opera House. It made the Condé Nast 'Hot' list for new hotels in 2007.

Phoenix Copenhagen

Bredgade 37; tel: 33 95 95 00; www.phoenixcopenhagen.dk; bus: 1a, 15, 19; €€€€

This is an elegant, deluxe hotel in an 18th-century mansion, close to the Royal Palace and Kongens Nytorv. All rooms and suites are air-conditioned and furnished elegantly in the French Louis XVI style.

Rosenborg and Around

Hotel Christian IV

Dronningens Tværgade 45; tel: 33 32 10 44; www.hotelchristianiv.dk; €€

A small, pleasant hotel located beside the lovely King's Garden (Kongens Have). Rooms are neat and bright, and fitted with modern Danish furniture;

Price for a standard double room for one night without breakfast in high season:

€€€€	over 1,600dkk
€€€	1,400–1,600dkk
€€	1,000–1,400dkk
€	under 1,000dkk

some quieter rooms overlook the inner courtyard. Guests have free entry to the gym round the corner on Adelsgade (www.fitnessdk.dk). There is free coffee, tea, fruit and cake available everyday from noon.

Axel Guldsmeden

Helgolandsgade 11; tel: 33 31 32 66; www.hotelguldsmeden.dk; €€€–€€€€

This new hotel is the fourth (and first four-star) hotel in the Guldmedsen group. Following in its sister-hotels' footsteps, it offers lovely, individual rooms decorated in colonial style – all the furniture here is made in Bali – as well as all mod-cons and delicious organic breakfasts.

The group prides itself on its socially responsible, eco-friendly and organic credentials. Its advantages over the other hotels in the group include being closer to the centre of town and, when the hotel is complete, having a wellness centre and pool on site.

Bertrams Guldsmeden

Vesterbrogade 107; tel: 33 25 04 05; www.hotelguldsmeden.dk; bus: 6a, 26; €€€

Carlton Guldsmeden

Vesterbrogade 66; tel: 33 22 15 00; www.hotelguldsmeden.dk; bus: 6a, 26; €€

These are both very charming hotels belonging to the same chain as the new Axel Guldsmeden. They are both a bit further down Vesterbrogade, which is fine to walk but a bus (these appear to be regular) or cab will be appealing if you have had a long day.

Best Western Hotel Hebron

Helgolandsgade 4; tel: 33 31 69 06; www.bestwestern.dk; €–€€
Comfortable, if unremarkable, but in a central position close to the station.

Cab Inn Copenhagen Express

Danasvej 32–34, Frederiksberg; tel: 33 21 04 00; www.cabinn.dk; €

Cab Inn Scandinavia

Vodroffsvej 55, Frederiksberg; tel: 35 36 11 11; www.cabinn.dk; €
Both of these hotels in the stylish and popular budget chain are located close to Peblinge Sø (Lake), approximately a 12-minute walk from Rådhuspladsen. You can sleep a family of four for under 1,000dkk. *(See also Cab Inn City, p.110.)*

Centrum

Helgolandsgade 14; tel: 33 31 31 11; www.dgi-byen.com/hotel; €
Formerly rather drab, this hotel has been renovated and is as a result significantly more light and airy. It is now part of the dgi-Byen group and guests have free entry to the dgi-Byen swimming centre and spa, 300m away and also benefit from a discount at the restaurant.

Copenhagen Crown

Vesterbrogade 41; tel: 33 21 21 66; www.profilhotels.dk; bus: 6a, 26; €
Newly updated and now part of the ProfilHotel group, this is a fresh,

Above from far left: stylish Front Hotel; do not disturb; the lobby in Front Hotel; the breakfast bar at the Axel Guldsmeden.

modern hotel, in the centre of things, with amenities for business travellers as well as holidaymakers.

Copenhagen Island

Kalvebod Brygghe 53; tel: 33 38 96 00; www.copenhagenisland.com; bus: 30; €–€€

Located on an artificial island in Copenhagen Harbour east of Vesterbro, this Arp-Hansen hotel opened in 2006. It offers all the mod cons, including a lovely restaurant, fitness centre with views over the harbour and flat-screen TVs in all the rooms. Depending on dates, a standard double room can be under 1,000dkk.

First Hotel

Vesterbrogade 23–29; tel: 33 78 80 00; www.firsthotels.dk/vesterbro; bus: 6a, 26; €€

First Hotel is centrally placed on Vesterbrogade and its attractive minimalist decor retains a sense of warmth, thanks perhaps to the cherry-wood furniture. All the rooms are a decent size and look down onto an internal, airy atrium where you have breakfast. In days of yore, it used to be the local porn cinema. It is run by the same group as the Sankt Petri hotel *(see p.113)*. Recommended in its price range.

Grand Hotel

Vesterbrogade 9a; tel: 33 27 69 00; www.grandhotel.dk; bus: 6a, 26; €€€

An attractive façade, dating from 1890, fronts another tasteful hotel belonging to the Arp-Hansen group.

It is centrally placed on a corner in uptown Vesterbro and in 2006 was carefully modernized in a manner that preserved much of its original character. Decor is in calming tones with splashes of accentuating colour.

Hotel dgi-Byens

Tietgensgade 65; tel: 33 29 80 50; www.dgi-byen.com; bus: 1a, 65e; €€

Close to Central Station and Tivoli, this recently opened hotel is comfortable and the decor Danish minimalist. It's very good for families and also conferences. The Vandkulturhuset, the city's state-of-the-art swimming complex and spa, is part of the hotel and guests have access to it.

Marriott Copenhagen

Kalvebod Brygge 5; tel: 88 33 99 00; www.marriott.com/cphdk; bus: 30; €€€

This hotel offers a waterside location with a lovely view through the huge glass windows on the harbour side; comfortable, good-sized rooms; a health spa; and all the mod cons and perks that you would expect from a five-star hotel. The only drawback is that it is on a main road, which makes

Price for a standard double room for one night without breakfast in high season:	
€€€€	over 1,600dkk
€€€	1,400–1,600dkk
€€	1,000–1,400dkk
€	under 1,000dkk

no difference when you are inside but makes getting places a little less straightforward on foot.

Mayfair Hotel

Helgolandsgade 3; tel: 70 12 17 00; www.choicehotels.dk/hotels/hotel?hotel=DK025&language=en; €€
An early 20th-century hotel that has recently been refurbished. It offers a cosy atmosphere with English-style decor and a good standard of service.

Norlandia Star Hotel

Colbjørnsensgade 13; tel: 33 22 11 00; www.norlandiahotels.dk; €–€€
This recently refreshed, functional and central hotel is reasonably priced (especially for double rooms and when booking online), although perhaps lacking in ambience.

Radisson Falconer Hotel

Falkoner Allé 9, Frederiksberg; tel: 38 15 80 01; www.radissonsas.com; bus: 18; €€
In a pleasant location near Copenhagen Zoo, just 2km (1 mile) west of the city centre, this is the smallest of the Copenhagen Radisson hotels. There is a tropical atrium lobby, a fitness centre and rooms in either Scandinavian, 'Oriental' or 'Art Deco' styles, most of which have a good view.

Copenhagen Suburbs

Hilton Copenhagen Airport Hotel

Ellehammersvej 20; tel: 32 50 15 01; www.hilton.com; €€–€€€€
Directly linked to Terminal 3, this five-star hotel recently won, for the fifth time, the award for Best Hotel in Denmark in the Copenhagen Area. It also has the largest rooms in the city and a brand new spa and wellness centre.

Hotel Fy & Bi

Valby Langgade 62, Valby; tel: 36 45 44 00; www.hotelfyogbi.dk; €
A charming 100-year-old building in traditional Danish yellow, offering modern facilities, a good restaurant and an excellent Danish breakfast buffet. The rooms lack character but the building and location – near the zoo and 10 minutes by bus or S-tog from the centre – make up for it.

Ocean Hotel

Amager Strandvej, Kastrup; tel: 27 27 02 03; www.oceanhotel.dk; €
A charming, beachside six-room hotel (with conference facilities) in a restored villa 7km (4 miles) from the centre and 1km (0.6 miles) from the airport. The rooms are large, attractive and airy (sleeping up to four) and there is a lovely garden, but no en-suite bathrooms.

Radisson Scandinavia Hotel

Amager Blvd 70; tel: 33 96 50 00; www.radissonsas.com; bus: 5a, 250s; €€€
On the island of Amager, this is Denmark's highest hotel at a towering 25-storeys high. Rooms are furnished in standard Scandinavian or 'Oriental' decor, most having fine views. It's convenient for the airport and there are four restaurants, including the recommended Blue Elephant.

Above from far left: the superb swimming pool at the Hilton Copenhagen Airport Hotel; many hotel rooms are a showcase for Danish design; the Hilton Copenhagen Airport Hotel; relaxing in style.

Staying in the Suburbs
The suburbs are not very far away and even if you stay out by the airport, you are only 15 minutes away from the centre by train.

RESTAURANTS

Café Ultimo

Tivoli; tel: 33 75 07 51; Sun–Thur
11am–midnight; Fri–Sat 11am–
12.30am (lunch: noon–4pm; dinner
5–10pm); €€–€€€

This Italian restaurant, housed in a
pretty, white glass structure, is not far
from Tivoli's lake and dates from 1883.
It offers such delicacies as pan-fried
foie gras with pear chutney and rucola
tossed in truffle oil as well as a good
selection of pasta dishes and pizzas.

Copenhagen Corner

Vesterbrogade 1A; tel: 33 91 45 45;
www.remmen.dk; daily 11.30am–
midnight; €–€€

This brightly decorated restaurant overlooking the Town Hall serves excellent
French/Danish cuisine. Specialities
include very good *smørrebrød* and fried
veal, garlic entrecôte and a herring plate
consisting of spiced and marinated herring with boiled potatoes.

Nimb

Berstorffsgade 5; tel: 88 70 00 00;
www.nimb.dk; €–€€€€

The wonderful Moorish Palace in Tivoli
has recently undergone an extensive
transformation, taking it back to the
original design of 1909. It is now a
gourmet heaven with a smart restaurant (€€€€) and a more informal,
family-friendly brasserie (€–€€) as
well as a delicatessen with its own
dairy, kitchen and chocolate production and an Italian-style wine cellar,
not to mention conference facilities
and a 12-room boutique hotel. Chef

Thomas Herman, formerly chef at the
Kong Hans Kælder restaurant, takes
Danish dishes and reinterprets them in
more modern style. For a quick snack
at a good price, the gourmet hotdog
stand serves up organic sausages in a
brioche bun with onions fried in duck's
fat and rosemary.

Pirateriet

Tivoli; tel: 33 75 07 20;
www.tivoligardens.com;
noon–Tivoli closing time; €–€€

What's more magical than eating your
victuals in a proper pirate ship, which
you enter over a gangplank? Formerly
Fregatten, a smart restaurant, this replica
sailing ship is now home to a new family
restaurant serving Caribbean food. Sit
in the galley, the captain's cabin or on
deck, and watch out for crocodiles!

Formel B

Vesterbrogade 182, Vesterbro; tel:
33 25 10 66; www.formel-b.dk;
Mon–Sat 6pm–1am, last table
reservation at 10pm; €€€€

A charming Michelin-starred restaurant where you can relax in a restful
interior decorated in shades of white,
chocolate and taupe. Eat à la carte or,
for 700dkk, sit down to a set menu of

Prices for an average three-course meal without wine:

€€€€	over 550dkk
€€€	400–550dkk
€€	250–400dkk
€	under 250dkk

six fabulous courses (not including wine). The menu changes every two weeks and offers dishes such as Danish cod with watercress, dandelion and cod roe; monkfish with snails, mushrooms and basil; and escalope of foie gras with kale and giblets. In summer, there's a terrace for outdoor dining.

Restaurant Klubben

Enghavevej 4; tel: 33 31 40 15; €
This pub is a little too rough and ready to tempt many tourists if they are not already in the know. However, if you are happy on wobbly tables with plastic table cloths and occasional beery-looking locals, this place offers generous portions of traditional home cooking such as *frikadeller* with creamed cabbage and beetroot or the traditional Danish plate of herring.

Fiasco

Gammel Kongevej 176, Frederiksberg; tel: 33 31 74 87; Tue–Sat 5.30–10pm; €€
This rustic, unpretentious Italian restaurant offers borderline gourmet dishes at reasonable prices. In the summer you can eat alfresco.

The Latin Quarter, Strøget and Around

Laszlo Café and Bar

Læderstræde 28; tel: 33 33 88 08; daily 11am–1am; €
Decent, hearty portions of Mediterranean-style sandwiches and salads with lots of sun-dried tomatoes. In season, you can happily eat outside on this appealing little street.

Restaurant Gråbrødre Torv 21

Gråbrødretorv 21; tel: 33 11 47 07; www.graabrodre21.aok.dk; daily lunch and dinner; €€€
Set in a lovely old house on an ancient square, it's worth the trip for the location alone. Danish fare is the speciality and is well prepared and presented.

Kobenhavner Kafeen

Badstruestræde 10; tel: 33 32 80 81; daily 10am–midnight; €–€€
This small restaurant has an old-time atmosphere and a traditional menu to go with it; *flæskesteg* (roasted pork, a Christmas speciality), *frikadeller* (meatballs), grilled plaice and a recommended cold table and daily 'Plate' of marinated salmon, herring, shrimp, meatballs, vegetables and baked bread for 150dkk.

Det Lille Apotek

Store Kannikestræde 15; tel: 33 12 56 06; www.det-lille-apotek.dk; Mon–Sat 11am–midnight, Sun noon–midnight; €–€€
The 'Little Pharmacy' is Copenhagen's oldest cellar restaurant, with crooked walls and antiques. It claims many writers as former customers, including Hans Christian Andersen and Ludvig Holberg. The food is mainly Danish, with plenty of hearty fish and meat dishes, including steak. Students love it.

Riz Raz

Kompanistræde 20; tel: 33 15 05 75; www.rizraz.dk; daily 11.30am–midnight; €
This attractive Mediterranean restaurant is very popular and offers an excellent

Karriere Contemporary Art & Social Life
Flaesketorvet 57–67; tel: 33 21 55 09; www.karrierebar.com; daily 7am–late; €€. New in November 2007, this experimental bar and restaurant in a former Vesterbro butchers' hall, is an interesting concept, seeking to 'give art an immediate relevance and meaning in an exclusive yet informal environment'. So check out its organic menu not to mention the bar counter, which moves from side to side, as well as other unusual works.

Badteåtret

In summer, the theatre boat on Nyhavn is a more charming and usually less crowded spot than any of the bars on the north side. It offers experimental theatre performances downstairs but if your Danish isn't up to it, sitting on deck with a glass in your hand is a very enjoyable way to spend the evening. Prices are not above average either.

Hviids Vinstue

Kongens Nytorv 19; tel: 33 15 10 64
Cosy, atmospheric and pub-like, Copenhagen's oldest wine bar dates from 1723. In winter, sit in the wood-panelled interior; in summer, sit outside. There is a smoking room if you don't want to brave the elements.

and varied vegetarian buffet. The cuisines of Lebanon, Morocco and Italy are all inspirations. There are some meat dishes for the more carnivorous.

Nouveau

Magstræde 16; tel: 33 16 12 92; www.restaurantnouveau.dk; Tues–Sat 6pm–2am; €€€€

Until 2007 a restaurant called *The Thief, the Cook, his Wife and her Lover*, occupied this lovely, 17th-century building. It has since been bought by the former head chef of Michelin-starred Kommandanten (now no longer trading) whose aim is to create a classic French meal with a unique modern touch. The set menu costs 690dkk and there is also a short à la carte menu, including dishes such as pot-au-feu of pigeon with truffles, sweetbreads and carrots; and salted tenderloin of pork with *ventrèche* served with poached leg of pork with rosemary and cranberries.

Kongens Nytorv, Nyhavn and Around

E-go

Hovedvagtsgade 2; tel: 33 12 79 71; www.egocph.dk; Mon–Thur 11.30am–midnight, Fri 11.30am–2am, Sat 10am–2am; €€–€€€

The classic French and Danish cuisine is carefully prepared and nicely presented in a trendy interior with a corrugated iron roof and interesting purple lighting. The staff are very helpful, the food good and, owing to its late opening, it's a popular place for a cocktail before heading out clubbing.

Nyhavns Færgekro

Nyhavn 5; tel: 33 15 15 88; www.nyhavnsfærgekro.dk; daily 9am–1pm; €–€€

An unpretentious restaurant set in an 18th-century building, serving particularly good traditional food, including *smørrebrød*, and a good herring buffet.

Restaurant Pierre André

Ny Østergade 21; tel: 33 16 17 19; Tue–Sat noon–2pm and 6–10pm; €€€€

This is an intimate, though quite formal, terracotta-walled restaurant offering delicious French gourmet food. There are two set menus at 675dkk and 820dkk; the latter consists of nine dishes created by the chef for the whole table and needs 20 hours notice. Sit back and enjoy.

Umami

Store Kongensgade 59; tel: 33 38 75 00; www.restaurantumami.dk; Mon–Fri noon–3pm, Sun–Thur 6–10pm, Fri–Sat 6–11pm; €€€€

Cool and very expensive, this stylish Japanese-French fusion restaurant is a popular celebrity haunt. There is a ground-floor cocktail bar and a sushi bar and restaurant upstairs serving dishes such as ginger-poached duck breast

Prices for an average three-course meal without wine:	
€€€€	over 550dkk
€€€	400–550dkk
€€	250–400dkk
€	under 250dkk

with gyoza, sesame and garlic; grilled sea bream with mushrooms and artichoke and cauliflower purée, white soya sauce, chili and coriander; and grilled veal tenderloin with wasabi and truffle sauce.

Custom House

Havnegade 44; tel: 33 31 01 30; www.customhouse.dk; Bacino: Mon–Fri 11.30am–2pm, Mon–Wed 5.30–10pm, Thur–Fri 5.30–11pm; €–€€€; Bar and Grill: Sun–Wed 11.30am–10pm, Thur–Sat 11.30am–11pm; €€; Ebisi Tue–Wed 5.30–10pm, Thur–Sat 5.30–11pm; €€–€€€

Overlooking the Sound is this new 'complex' of Conran eateries and bars housed in a building built in 1937 in a functionalist 'jazz-modern' style. Choose between Bacino, offering traditional seasonal fare in a creamy-white interior, a bar and grill offering hearty Danish-European dishes and Ebisu, a Japanese grill and sushi bar, where the 10-dish menu costs 575dkk. There are also two bars open until late.

Rosenborg and Around

Den Grønne Kælder

Pilestræde 48; tel: 33 93 01 40; Mon–Sat 11am–10pm; €

One of Copenhagen's few vegetarian restaurants, this is an excellent place for a wholesome meal, including a good selection of vegan options. Czech and organic beer are both on offer.

Kokkeriet

Kronprinsessegade 64; tel: 33 15 27 77; www.kokkeriet.dk; Tue–Sat 6pm–1am; €€€€

This charming, relaxed modern restaurant boasts one Michelin star and a monthly changing six-course set menu offering beautifully presented, interesting food combinations: scallops in buttermilk, with cabbage and malt; foie gras giblets, apples and cowberry; filet of lamb with celeriac, mushrooms and sherry sauce; and carrot ice cream with lychee and liquorice. You can also eat à la carte and arrange to take lessons from the chef!

Kong Hans Kælder

Vingaardstræde 6; tel: 33 11 68 68; www.konghans.dk; Mon–Sat 6pm–midnight; €€€€

Set in Copenhagen's oldest building, this structure is mentioned in medieval texts. In the 19th century, Hans Christian Andersen lived in its garret. Now a Michelin-starred, expensive treat, it's one of the most splendid venues in the city. The food is French-influenced with an emphasis on simplicity and fresh ingredients and features roasted langoustines from Kattegat with black salsifys and brown-butter and sea-berry vinaigrette; glazed turbot with rosehip and *marjolaine*, ceps, chestnuts and Jerusalem artichokes; gooseleg confit and foie gras with local apples and Danish apple balsamic vinegar.

Restaurant Godt

Gothersgade 38; tel: 33 15 21 22; www.restaurant-godt.dk; Tue–Sat 6pm–midnight, closed July; €€€€

Godt means 'good', something of an understatement for this family-run, 20-seat restaurant. The cuisine is

Above from far left: refreshing drinks; traditional open sandwich; Japanese food is popular with the young hip crowd; asparagus with a Danish twist.

Fixed Menus
Many restaurants have fixed-price menus and the greater the number of courses, proportionately the cheaper your meal becomes. If you are on more of a budget, eat in a café where a couple of unpretentious courses will set you back 150–200dkk or try out the *pølsevogn*, sausage vans that you will find all over town. Also, bear in mind that alcohol is expensive, especially in restaurants.

Kontiki Bar

Takkelloftvej 1z
v/operahuset; tel: 29
46 54 17; open daily
until late; €.

If the stylish bar/
restaurant at the
opera house doesn't
appeal, head for this
rough-and-ready boat
just behind it. The
menu is not extensive
and changes at the
whim of the chef. Not
sophisticated but
charming – especially
on a summer evening.

European with one daily three- to five-course seasonal menu; the wine list is mainly French. It has one Michelin star, so reservations are advised.

Restaurationen

Møntergade 19; tel: 33 14 94 95;
www.restaurationen.com; Tue–Sat
6pm–midnight; €€€€

Multiple award-winning Restaurationen has won just about every star that magazine and food writers have to give, including Michelin and the Wine Spectator award of excellence. Its distinctive six-course fixed menu (700dkk), based on Danish, French and Italian cuisine, is revised every week, with dishes using fresh, seasonal produce. Its decor is traditional with contemporary touches.

San Giorgio

Rosenborggade 7 (near the Kultorvet);
tel: 33 12 61 20; www.san-giorgio.dk;
Mon–Sat 6–11pm; €€–€€€

Nicely decorated with white-washed walls, dark wood furniture, chandeliers, candles and crisp white tablecloths, San Giorgio offers authentic Italian cuisine that is very much more than just pizza and pasta. Three fixed menus give you a choice on price.

St Gertrude's Kloster

Hauserplads 32; tel: 33 14 66 30;
daily 5–11pm; €€€€

This lovely restaurant can be found within the atmospheric walls of a 14th-century monastery. Begin with an aperitif in the leather-book-lined library before repairing to the candlelit vault to eat fabulous food based on medieval recipes, including foie gras that melts on the tongue.

Ankara

Krystalgade 8; tel: 33 15 19 15;
www.restaurant-ankara.dk; Mon–Sat
1pm–midnight; €

Extensive Turkish buffet-style eaterie adapted for Danish tastes; a belly dancer provides the entertainment.

Amalienborg and Around

Le Sommelier

Bredgade 63-65; tel: 33 11 45 15;
www.lesommelier.dk; Mon–Thur
noon–2pm and 6–10pm, Fri noon–
2pm and 6–11pm, Sat 6–11pm,
Sun 6–10pm; €€€–€€€€

A charming French restaurant, it prides itself on being Copenhagen's 'first genuine wine bar'. It reputedly has the largest cellar in Denmark, offering wine by the bottle or by the glass, which is not always as expensive as you might expect. The food is delicious (approach the *assiette tout chocolat* with an open waistband) and its two-course lunch menu costs a reasonable 270dkk, while the three-course evening menu is 385dkk. The menu changes but expect lamb, beef, pork, duck, foie gras and fresh fish in a variety of interesting dishes.

Prices for an average three-course meal without wine:

€€€€	over 550dkk
€€€	400–550dkk
€€	250–400dkk
€	under 250dkk

Slotsholmen and South of Strøget

Slotskælderen

Fortunstræde 4; tel: 33 11 15 37;
Tue–Sat 10am–5pm; €–€€
This is a small restaurant dating from 1910 and much favoured by politicians from the nearby parliament who enjoy their excellent open sandwiches and Danish menu, including home-cured herring and home-brewed *snaps*.

Sorgenfri

Brolæggerstræde 8; tel: 33 11 58 80;
daily 11am–9pm; €
This 150-year-old *frokost* restaurant tucked in a basement just north of Christiansborg Castle is not posh but, for a very Danish fast-food eatery, it has good *smørrebrød*, beer and *snaps*.

Rio Bravo

Vester Voldgade 86; tel: 33 11 75 87;
www.riobravo.dk; daily 11.30pm–5am, Sun from 5pm; €–€€
This popular place is a favourite among late-night revellers. It's a no-nonsense, cowboy-style steakhouse, where even the seats at the bar are saddles.

Christianshavn and Holmen

Era Ora

Overgaden Neden Vandet 33B;
tel: 32 54 06 93; www.era-ora.dk;
Mon–Sat lunch noon–3pm, dinner 7pm–1am (kitchen closes 11.30pm);
€€€–€€€€
This friendly Michelin-starred, stylish Italian restaurant by the canal has a calming, Italianate, beige-and-white interior and a pretty summer court-yard. Era Ora serves innovative Italian cuisine and is considered one of the best restaurants in the city. Lunch is less costly than dinner.

Noma

Strandgade 93, Nordatlantens Brygghe, Christianshavn; tel: 32 96 32 97; www.noma.dk; €€€€
One of the city's newest gourmet restaurants, Noma occupies an 18th-century warehouse near the docks. It takes its inspiration, both in terms of decor and cuisine, from Denmark, Ice-land, Greenland and the Faroe islands from where it imports its fresh in-gredients every day. The chef conjures up dishes such as bouillon of birch wine and mushrooms, chickweed and egg yolk; and reindeer and celery, woodruff and ramson onion capers, and has earnt two Michelin stars. For the experience without the top-end ex-pense, come for the three-course lunch menu (325dkk). In the evening, a seven-course menu is on offer, which, at 800dkk, is still rather good value.

Nørrebro

KiinKiin

Guldbergsgade 21; tel: 35 35 75 55
(for takeaways: 35 35 95 05 55);
www.kiin.dk; Mon–Sat 6pm–midnight;
€€€€
The name is an exhortation to 'come and eat!', and it's hard to turn down this rising star on the Copenhagen gourmet scene. It offers a daily menu of five modern Thai courses in a lovely ambi-ence. Also check out its takeaway menu at a reasonable 45–95dkk per dish.

Above from far left: wine by the glass; presentation is of the essence; Noma, the only two-starred Michelin restaurant in Copenhagen; a feast for the eyes.

CREDITS

Insight Step by Step Copenhagen
Written by: Antonia Cunningham
Series Editor: Clare Peel
Managing Editor: Carine Tracanelli
Cartography: James Macdonald/Zoë Goodwin
Picture Manager: Steven Lawrence
Photography by: Apa/Rudy Hemmingsen except:
4Corners 8-1, 60-2, 63-1; AKG 49-3; Axel Gulds-
meden 27-1, 114-2, 115-2, 121-1; Bridgeman Art
Library 63-2 © Succession H Matisse/DACS 2008;
Camerapress 32-1, 72-1; Carlsberg 28-2, 29-1, 29-3,
29-4, 31-1; Antonia Cunningham 65-1; Design
Hotels 40-1; Experimentarium 95-2, 95-3, 95-4;
Front 36-3, 98-4, 98-5, 114-1, 115-1; Getty Images
11-1; Hotel 27 15-3, 27-3, 38-4, 40-2, 98-1, 98-3,
112-2, 113-1, 116-2, 118-1, 119-1, 122-1; Hotel Fox
110/111 (all); iStockphoto.com 2-1, 2-2, 2-5, 2-6,
4-2, 8-2, 8-4, 8-7, 10-1, 12-3, 13-2, 14-2, 14-5, 16-1,
16-2, 18-1, 22-1, 23-1, 24-1, 24-2, 24-5, 44-2, 45-4,
51-1, 51-2, 53-1, 55-2, 55-3, 58-4, 67-1, 67-3, 70 (all),
74-1, 77-2, 85-3, 88-1, 89-2, 90-3, 90-4, 92-2, 100,
101, 103-1, 106, 108-1, 109 (all); 118-2, 120-2;
Leonard 19-1, 26-1, 40-4, 43-3, 98-2, 98-7, 112-1,
113-2; Museum Erotica 38-3, 39-1; Rex Features 41-
2; Rust 20-2, 20-3, 21-2; SEIER+SEIER 24-4; SMK
Foto 60-1, 60-3, 60-4, 62-2, 64 (all); Tycho Brahe
Planetarium 66-2; VEGA 21-1; VisMedia 116-1, 117
(all); Wonderful Copenhagen 10-2, 10-3, 13-3, 14-1,
14-3, 14-4, 15-1, 15-2, 16-3, 16-4, 17-1, 18-2, 18-3,
19-2, 19-3, 27-2, 28-1, 28-3, 32-2, 32-3, 36-2, 37-1,
37-4, 40-3, 43-1, 44-3, 45-5, 46 (all), 47-1, 49-1, 50-2,
59-3, 66-1, 67-2, 81-3, 97-1, 97-2, 97-4, 98-6, 102
(all), 107, 119-2, 120-1, 121-2, 122-2, 123 (all).
Front Cover: main image Getty Images; bottom left
C.B Poulsen/Wonderful Copenhagen; bottom right
Apa/Rudy Hemmingsen.

Printed by: Insight Print Services (Pte) Ltd, 38 Joo
Koon Road, Singapore 628990.

© 2008 Apa Publications GmbH & Co.
Verlag KG (Singapore branch)

All rights reserved

First Edition 2008

www.insightguides.com

DISTRIBUTION

Worldwide
Apa Publications GmbH & Co. Verlag KG (Singapore branch), 38 Joo Koon Road, Singapore 628990
Tel: (65) 6865 1600
Fax: (65) 6861 6438

UK and Ireland
GeoCenter International Ltd
Meridian House, Churchill Way West, Basingstoke, Hampshire, RG21 6YR
Tel: (44) 01256 817 987
Fax: (44) 01256 817 988

United States
Langenscheidt Publishers, Inc.
36–36 33rd Street, 4th Floor, Long Island City, NY 11106
Tel: (1) 718 784 0055
Fax: (1) 718 784 0640

Australia
Universal Publishers
1 Waterloo Road, Macquarie Park, NSW 2113
Tel: (61) 2 9857 3700
Fax: (61) 2 9888 9074

New Zealand
Hema Maps New Zealand Ltd (HNZ)
Unit D, 24 Ra ORA Drive, East Tamaki, Auckland
Tel: (64) 9 273 6459
Fax: (64) 9 273 6479

CONTACTING THE EDITORS

We would appreciate it if readers would alert us to errors or outdated information by writing to us at insight@apaguide.co.uk or Apa Publications, PO Box 7910, London SE1 1WE, UK.

INDEX

Copenhagen M

Vanløse · Flintholm · Lindevang · Solbjerg · Frederiksberg · Forum · Nørreport · Kongens Nytorv · Christianshavn · Amagerbro · Lergravsparken · Øresund · Amager Strand · Femøren · Kastrup · Lufthavnen/Airport · M2

Islands Brygge · Universitetet · Sundby · Bella Center · Ørestad · Vestamager · M1

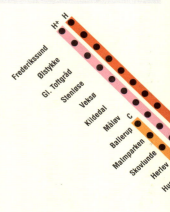

H+ H
Frederikssund · Ølstykke · Gl. Toftgård · Stenløse · Veksø · Kildedal · Måløv · C · Ballerup · Malmparken · Skovlunde · Herlev · Hus

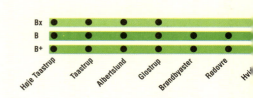

Bx
B
B+
Høje Taastrup · Taastrup · Albertslund · Glostrup · Brøndbyøster · Rødovre · Hvi

●	Interchange Station	
A	Hillerød - Hundige	
A+	Østerport - Køge	
B	Holte - Høje Taastrup	
B+	Holte - Høje Taastrup	
Bx	Klampenborg - Høje Taastrup	
C	Klampenborg - Ballerup	
E	Hillerød - Køge	
Ex	Hellerup - Køge	
F,F+	Klampenborg - Ny Ellebjerg	
H	Farum - Frederikssund	
H+	Farum - Frederikssund	

Copenhagen S-tog (S-train)